A Travelguide to Slickrock Bike Trail and
Mountain Biking Adventures.

Published by Mountain N' Air Books
P.O. Box 12540
La Crescenta, CA 91224

Title: **MOAB, Utah**

Published in the United States of America by
Mountain N'Air Books - P.O. Box 12540 - La Crescenta, CA 91224
Phone: (818) 951-4150, fax: (818) 951-4153

Cover design and book layout by Gilberto d'Urso
All photographs were taken by the author, unless otherwise credited.

Library of Congress Cataloguing-in-Publication Data

Ward, Bob.
Moab, Utah: a travelguide to Slickrock Bike Trail and mountain biking adventures / by Bob Ward.
p. cm.
Includes bibliographical references (p.) and index.
ISBN 1-879415-11-9
1. All terrain cycling – Utah – Slickrock Bike Trail – Guidebooks. 2. All terrain cycling – Utah – Moab – Guidebooks. 3. Outdoor recreation – Utah – Moab – Guidebooks. 4. Slickrock Bike Trail (Utah)– Guidebooks. 5. Moab (Utah) – Guidebooks. I. Title.
GV1045.5.U82S559 1995
796.6'4'09792– dc20 95-5687
CIP

ISBN: 1-879415-11-9

Acknowledgments

The author would like to thank the following people for contributing in some way toward the creation of this travel guide. First and foremost, my wife Annie, my favorite bike buddy and initial proof reader. Gilberto d'Urso of Mountain N' Air Books for recognizing the need for this book and for taking care of the publishing end. Crack ace mechanic Jim Lowe who joined me on my first Moab road trip and has kept my bikes rolling in top shape for the past 10 years. Tharyn "shoe goo" Henderson, who has kept me amused on four Moab adventures. Chuck Pannell for his help and patience on the "research" tour. And to all my bike buddies that have shared the Moab experience with me - Dr. J, Uncle Joe, Carmen, Dennis, Ken, Kansas, Jackie, Susan, Mike, Kevin, Heath, Will, Craig, Trisa, Bobby D, Tom, Candayce, Dave, James don't call me Jimmy and the kids, Emo and Tess. The folks at Kaibab, especially guides Jimmy and Maggie, for a wonderful time on the White Rim Trail. All the Moab bike shops for helping to keep our bikes on line. Finally, all the great people in Moab that I met during my visits and while researching this book.

N
W
E
S
UTAH
Brigham City
Ogden
Bountiful
80
SALT
LAKE
CITY
Provo
15
Price
70
Richfield
Moab
Cedar City
9
Kanab
St. George
191
Page
COLORADO
Fort Colins
70
Boulder
Golden
DENVER
Grand Junction
50
Montrose
550
666
Durango
ARIZONA
NEW MEXICO

U.S. DEPARTMENT OF THE INTERIOR
BUREAU OF LAND MANAGEMENT
MOAB SLICKROCK
Bike Trail

You are here.

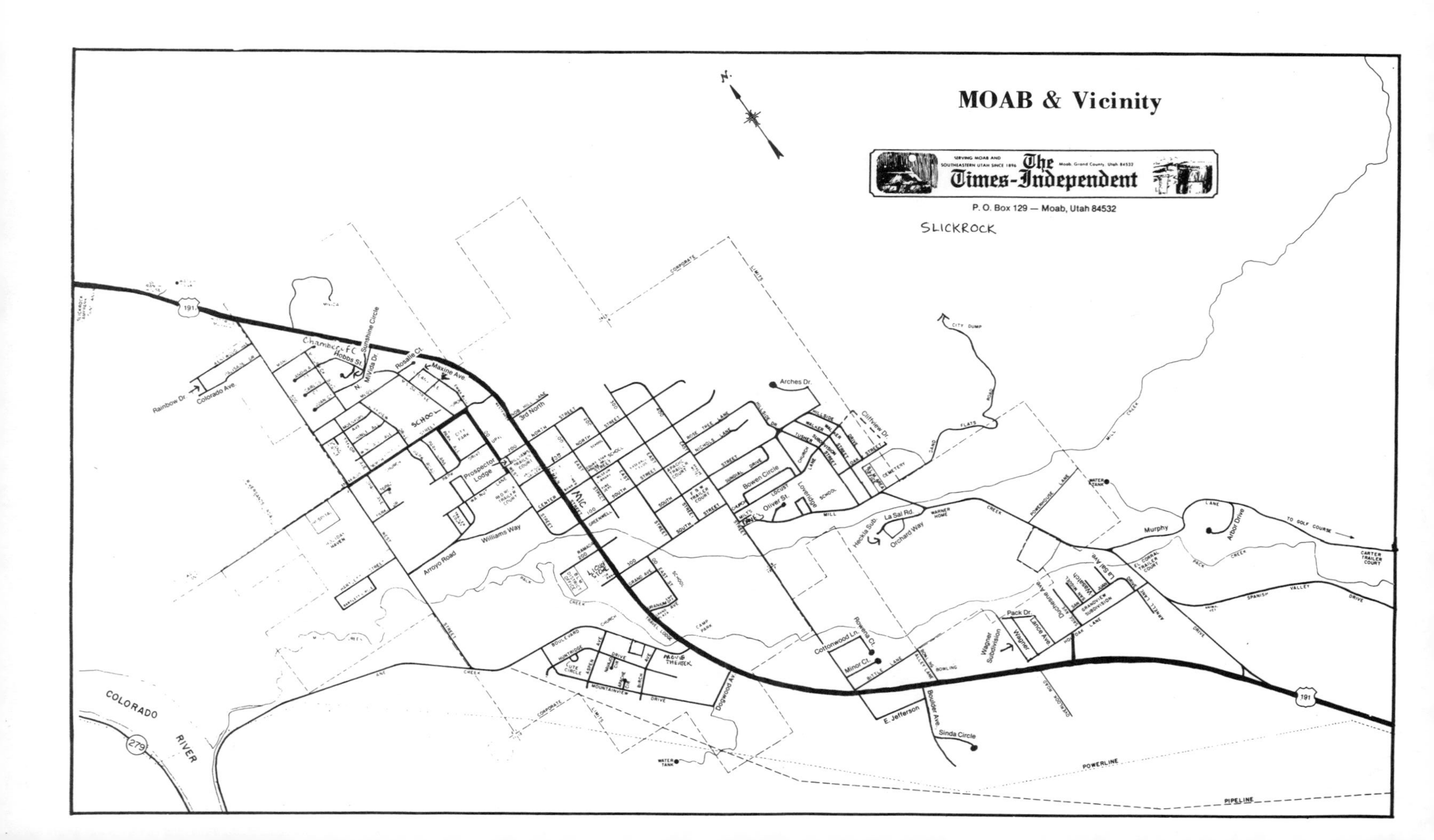
MOAB & Vicinity
SERVING MOAB AND SOUTHEASTERN UTAH SINCE 1896
The Times-Independent
Moab, Grand County, Utah 84532
P. O. Box 129 — Moab, Utah 84532
SLICKROCK
N.
CITY DUMP
Arches Dr.
Cliffview Dr.
CEMETERY
TO GOLF COURSE
CARTER TRAILER COURT
Arbor Drive
Murphy
LANE
WATER TANK
POWERHOUSE LANE
MILL CREEK
EL CORRAL TRAILER COURT
PACK CREEK
SPANISH VALLEY DRIVE
La Sal Ave.
Wasatch
Duchesne Ave.
GRANDVIEW SUBDIVISION
HOLYOAK LANE
Pack Dr.
Lance Ave.
Wagner
Wagner Subdivision
OVERLOOK ROAD
191
Rowena Ct.
Cottonwood Ln.
Minor Ct.
BITTLE LANE
ALLEY LANE
BOWLING
E. Jefferson
Boulder Ave.
Sinda Circle
POWERLINE
PIPELINE
Heckla Sub.
La Sal Rd.
Orchard Way
WARNER HOME
Loveridge
SCHOOL
Oliver St.
LOCUST
Bowen Circle
SUNDIAL DRIVE
HILLSIDE DR
ROSE TREE LANE
NICHOLS LANE
3rd North
Maxine Ave.
Rosalie Ct.
N. MiVida Dr.
Sunshine Circle
Hobbs St.
Chambers FC
Rainbow Dr.
Colorado Ave.
SCHOOL
CITY PARK
Prospector Lodge
Williams Way
Arroyo Road
BLM DISTRICT OFFICE
GRAND AVE
EAST ST
CAMP PARK
TRAVEL LODGE
BOULEVARD
HUNTRIDGE
CUTE CIRCLE
ASPEN AVE
MOUNTAINVIEW DRIVE
BIRCH AVE
MOVIE THEATER
Dogwood Av.
CORPORATE LIMITS
WATER TANK
COLORADO RIVER
279
191

Table of Contents

Welcome to Moab.

Introduction

By the time I finally got around to taking my first mountain bike road trip to southeastern Utah in the spring of 1988, Moab had already been dubbed by *Mountain Bike for the Adventure* magazine as the "Mountain Biker's Mecca." Since I have a firm belief that almost all writers tend to exaggerate, a claim like this could not be taken for granted. I felt it was my duty to check the validity of this coveted label first hand. So with buds Jimbo and Jar Head, we set out on a pilgrimage to what was rapidly becoming the most well known mountain bike destination in the country, if not the world.

Up to this point in my life I was a mountain man by heart. My most pleasurable moments tended to occur while at the higher elevations surrounded by lush forests or the alpine tundra. For me, this was going to be totally new — the desert experience that I had only been exposed to through the writings of Edward Abbey.

So what did I think? On all accounts, this was truly an enlightening experience. I instantly fell in love with the desert environment. It was certainly different from the mountains, and new concepts had to be taken into consideration, but I felt very comfortable despite my lack of experience.

The biking? As far as the actual riding was concerned, I had certainly been on better singletrack and jeep roads, but never had I biked in an area where the sheer raw beauty was so continuous. I often describe the Moab sights as a form of "sensory overload", as awe-inspiring vistas wait behind every bend in the road. Over the past six years and numerous visits, I have not come close to getting tired of setting my eyes upon the vast red rock canyons, unique sandstone formations, seas of slickrock fins and towering pillars. All framed, I might add, by the majestic La Sal Mountains.

The mountain bike experience? I was also amazed at how this magical spot had succeeded in luring mountain bikers from all over the world. While researching my first *Mountain Biking in the Northern Sierra* guidebook in 1986-7, I came across a total of two other bikers on the trails. Laying down first tracks was not so difficult. By 1988, biker sightings were up, but it was still more the exception rather than the rule. Moab was a definite exception. I remember giving my girl friend, Annie, a call from the old City Market and expressing to her the wonderful feeling of camaraderie I was experiencing in this town with hundreds of other mountain bikers.

Fast forward to the spring of 1994, and I am calling my wife, Annie, this time from the new City Market, and I was still impressed to be sharing this experience with not hundreds, but literally thousands of fellow mountain bikers. While hanging on the phone I gazed out to a sea of Yakima racks loaded with mountain bikes. License plates from just about every state in the Union were represented as well as most Canadian provinces. A foreign legion of bikers were exiting the market speaking in French, German and Spanish.

At this point, I was truly convinced that Moab wasn't just a mountain biker's Mecca but it had become the center of the mountain biker's universe. As far as mountain bikers are concerned, all roads and trails lead to Moab.

Since my first Moab tour, I have been back at least once every year. I have also given numerous slide presentations featuring Moab at bike shops and club meetings. There are always a few Moabsters in the audience who nod in agreement now and then when I mention some great spot that they have also biked. However, the majority of the audiences are usually filled with bikers who have yet to feel the red dirt or firm sandstone slickrock under their tires. After each program many of these unenlightened types are ready to begin planning their pilgrimage. Consequently, I never fail to get the twenty questions after the program. How do you get there? Where can you camp? Are there any cheap motels? Good restaurants? Where can I get maps or guidebooks? Is there a bike shop? Should I bring my own beer? These are just a few of the regular questions prompted the researching and writing of this book.

Armed with this guidebook, you should have absolutely no problem planning and executing your journey to the center of the mountain biker's universe. Do I describe the actual trails? No, but within these pages I will steer you toward the best of the guidebooks, the most detailed maps and the tour companies that can assist you on the trail. The rest is up to you. Read, plan, journey and enjoy. Happy Trails.

Another Slickrock Playground.

Taking a break, and the view on the White Rim.

The La Sal Mountains - a beautiful backdrop for most Moab.

Candlestick Butte along the White Rim.

Slickrock Trail

Slickrock playground along the Potash Road

The author and family taking a 'Power-Bar' break.

Checking out Bull Canyon, from Gemini Bridges

Descending from Boren Mesa in the La Sals Mountain.

Riding on Slickrock

What's All The Fuss About Moab?

Moab! The mere mention of the name usually conjures up positive images for most mountain bikers. With mass quantities of exposure or in some opinions, overexposure, in books, magazines, videos, advertisements and even "Tread the Movie," you would be hard pressed to find a mountain biker that has not heard of this classic mountain bike destination. This wasn't always the case.

Many years ago, before I discovered the joys of mountain biking, my only experience with Moab occurred as I drove through through the town returning from the Grand Canyon. While I was able to glimpse some of the splendor as I sped along the highway, I also considered the surreal landscape as harsh and unforgiving. I thought to myself that this was not the sort of place to experience on foot, which at the time was my prime mode of transportation in the backcountry when there wasn't snow on the ground.

In May of 1985 I purchased my first mountain bike. After a few rides I was hopelessly addicted to the sport. It wasn't long afterwards that Moab entered my realm of conscienceness as more than just a town to pass through, but as a special mountain bike destination.

Within a few weeks of the bike purchase I came across the premier issue of *Mountain Bike for the Adventure* magazine. I quickly snatched it up and read it cover to cover. I also spent an inordinate amount of time gazing at the front/back cover photo that was taken on a slickrock ridge overlooking Moab and the Colorado River. Within the pages were two particular articles that captured my attention.

The first was by Richard Compton titled "*Slickrock*". Richard's photos and story covered the gamut of slickrock riding, but the main focus was on riding the Slickrock Trail. I must have re-read the article five or six times over the following months which became my inspiration for eventually planning my first Moab road trip. Just as the petrified sand dunes that make up the slickrock seem to be frozen in time, Richard's description of the trail and his tips have also withstood the test of time. I have yet to read an article since that has captured the essence of the slickrock experience so well.

The second article was *"Cycling the Canyon Country"* by *Mountain Bike* editor Hank Barlow. While Richard's article was more matter of fact - this is how it is and this is how to ride it, Hank caught my attention with his rendering of the spirit of the canyon country experience. My favorite line from the article has managed to sum up much of how I feel. "The desert/canyon country is like a Japanese poem where much is said and felt with but a few words."

It has almost been a decade since these words were written and more has been said and written about Moab than any other single mountain bike destination. I know I have certainly contributed my share. But nobody else's words can quite prepare you for what you will find in canyon country. If you have been there, you should know what I mean. If you haven't, then it is about time you experience for yourself the scenic wonders, the biking challenges and the spiritual escape of the desert landscape.

Yes, there are other equally impressive mountain bike destinations, so why choose Moab? My feeling is this. There are thousands of great places to ride, but there is only one Moab. Due to the combination of its unique mountain biking and all of the ensuing publicity that it has received over the past decade, Moab has developed a mystique that no other region has come close to duplicating. Due to a combination of its intrinsic merits mixed generously with the hype that has come its way, Moab has, for better or worse, become the center of the mountain biker's universe. A trip to Moab is more than a mountain bike vacation; it is a pilgrimage to the mountain biker's Mecca.

For many, once will be enough. They came, they saw, they rode. Did it. Been there. For others, it will be the beginning of a spiritual awakening that will cause them to not only return, but to feel the urge to share the experience with others. There is only one Moab. And it must be seen, felt, and ridden to be fully appreciated.

I have made a point of returning to this area at least once a year since my first visit. A Moab road trip always serves to recharge my batteries. If I go in the spring, it usually serves the purpose of kicking off another great year of biking. If I save my visit for the fall, it puts an exclamation point at the end of another outstanding season.

On the other hand, it certainly isn't the only place to go for a mountain bike vacation. Variety is the spice of life and I make a point of going on a least one road trip each year to some other fine locale. I have found better trails with incredible singletrack, but I keep coming back.

For most readers of this book, there will be an almost unlimited supply of destinations closer to home that you could visit on your vacation. But there is only one Moab. Come - see - ride - experience it. Once you have **been there** and **done it**, then you will know what it is all about.

Facing up to the Backlash

Over the course of the past year, there has actually been some Moab backlash and occasional bad press. Much of this backlash has come from riders who have yet to sample the treats that Moab has to offer. The problem often stems from the fact that Moab has gotten too much publicity. With fame comes criticism.

Here are some of the most frequently heard complaints about Moab followed by my response.

- ✯ There are not any chair lifts so that we can do our gonzo downhill thing without climbing. *That is good in my book, let's hope it stays that way. While a lift can be appreciated, the best descents will always be ones that are earned.*

- ✯ There are too many other bikers and I don't like crowds. *Yes, indeed, masses of mountain bikers descend on Moab every year. If you can't deal with the masses, then I suggest you avoid the peak months.* I have found that even during the busiest times, that you can still find a taste of solitude by biking some of the routes that are further from town and/or getting a sunrise start.

- ✯ The Moab scene is overrated. *Who cares about ratings. Your experience should be between you and the canyon country.*

- ✯ Too much has been written about Moab. *The truth is, you can't say enough about this place.*

- ✯ Moab is only for advanced riders. *Definitely <u>not</u> true. Moab has rides that can accommodate all levels or riders.*

- There ar not enough singletracks. *Very true.* This is a valid negative point concerning Moab. If you have in mind a singletrack experience, you'd do better by going elsewhere.

  On the other hand, I know many bikers, including myself, that love singletrack and have yet to miss it while enjoying the rugged jeep trails of southeastern Utah.

- Some of the local non-biker types hassle mountain bikers. A recent article in BIKE magazine brought this to our attention as a couple were harassed while camping along Sand Flats Road. After checking with the local police, I found that this was more the exception rather than the rule. Almost any small town will have a few ya-whos with IQs below the average night temperature that occasionally get bored with their beer drinking and proceed to make asses out of themselves. One of these days they will hassle the wrong person and be sorry. In the meantime, don't spend any time worrying about this.

Riding on the Slickrock Bike Trails

The Determination Towers.

Moab for Everyone

On several occasions I have talked to folks after presentations on Moab who were initially under the impression that Moab was just for advanced riders. This could not be further from the truth. One major appeal of Moab is that there are tours for riders of all ability levels.

Although there are several rides that beginners might find over their heads, there are still many great rides novice mountain bikers can enjoy. The majority of the rides in the area are on jeep trails, many of which are not very technical. There are also many rides that do not require quantities of climbing. I'm not going to say that the rides are flat, which is never the case with mountain biking, but compared to biking in the mountains of the western states, most of the elevation gains and loses are minimal.

Intermediates will marvel at the vast selection of options at their disposal. I think that an intermediate rider in decent shape armed with a good attitude can probably complete just about any ride the region has to offer. Sure, you will find yourself portaging over some of the tougher sections, but you should be able to finish the rides.

If anything, some advanced riders might feel that there isn't enough singletrack to satisfy their needs. The lack of singletrack is perhaps the biggest knock on Moab. If, indeed, you desire miles and miles of singletrack, Moab may not be what you are looking for. However, if you like highly technical terrain with scenery that won't quit, then this is the place.

A beginners guide

Yes, you will have fun biking in Moab, I can almost guarantee it. The key is to only bike off what you can chew. Start with some of the easier rides and work your way up.

One of the biggest mistakes many a beginner makes is that either by choice or coercion, he or she begins Moab riding with a jaunt on the Slickrock Trail. An experienced biking buddy tells you it is only 12 miles and that it will be a snap. You are then led on the ride from hell. You are off your bike more than you are on, the fear factor has added a few gray hairs to your temples, and you crash and burn more times than you can remember. Heck, you don't even remember when you cracked your helmet, and you are wondering what in the hell are you doing in Moab as you crawl back to the trailhead utterly exhausted. You then proceed to spend the rest of your stay recovering from this "warm-up" ride.

Let me tell you, no visit to Moab is complete without at least a little time at the Slickrock Trail, but you don't need to ride it first thing. You don't have to complete the whole trail. And you sure don't have to rip through it at some gonzo racer's pace from hell.

Relax, you are on vacation. When you get to town, read over Todd Campbell's *Above and Beyond Slickrock* or talk to some of the knowledgeable folks at the bike shops and come up with some "doable rides" to ease into the experience.

One favorite "get the kinks out from the drive" ride is the cruise up to Hurrah Pass. Sure, there are some climbs (you can't get around that, but they are not very long), the road surface is totally non-technical, there are several petroglyphs to stop at and contemplate (they make for a good excuse to take a long break), and the view from the pass is well worth the price of admission.

You can work the Slickrock Trail into your schedule later in your stay, or better yet, give it a sample run after one of the easier rides. Get up early and do one of the non-technical tours to satisfy your urge to cover some miles. You should finish up early, so head back to your room or camp for some kick-back time. Later in the afternoon, drive on up to the Slickrock Trail and give it a whirl. Don't plan on doing the whole thing, just go on out and play. Follow the little white lines or go wherever you want. Mostly, take it easy, but occasionally push yourself on tougher sections. Learn what you can or can't do. You will be amazed at how quickly your "can do" limit expands.

If you have time and energy, you might want to complete the practice loop. Remember, that just because it is called the practice loop does not mean it is easy. In fact, it is just a short version of the full trail with the same technical challenges. Finally, always remember that there is no harm in walking your bike.

Some other rides you might want to put on your list of "must do and can do" rides include Monitor and Merrimac (Definitely take the side trip to the Determination Towers. I could have spent hours laz'n in the shade between the towers.), Gemini Bridges, Klondike Bluffs, Potash Road; and if you consider that your skills and endurance have improved, shoot for the Poison Spider Mesa tour as your climax to the trip.

Intermediates

Now, there are intermediates and there are intermediates. Some intermediates are only in this category for a short time as they go on to become advanced riders. For them, a week in Moab will probably do the trick. There are also what we refer to as terminal intermediates. These folks are content to enjoy a good ride without any pretensions about becoming the next Tomac or Hans Rey. Whether you are terminal or transitory, you will find that you can do just about any ride in the region. You might want to modify the ride a bit to accommodate your ability level, but you should be able to pick and choose just about any ride in Above and Beyond Slickrock.

Even though you have the skill and endurance over most beginners, I recommend that you also ease into the Moab scene. For most of us, Moab time begins after a lengthy road trip which can be a numbing experience for both bodies and minds. Consequently, when you arrive in town, take on a tour that will work out the kinks rather than add new ones. Although Moab isn't exactly the high country, it is still situated at 4000 feet and a day of acclimatizing will do you wonders and make the rest of your rides much more enjoyable.

Completing the Slickrock Trail should be on the list of any first time Moab intermediate rider. You don't, however, have to kill yourself doing it. I advise you to get an early start and go at a pace that is comfortable for you. If you are with some hard-core riders, let them go ahead at their pace and you stick to yours. One positive aspect of the popularity of the trail is that you will not be left alone and you might even meet some new friends along the way.

Some other great rides that an intermediate might want to chalk up include Poison Spider Mesa, Amasa Back, and if you are looking for a challenge to end your trip with, try the Porcupine Rim Trail. This is considered an advanced ride, but you can shorten it with a shuttle if need be. Porcupine Rims features a goodly climb, the longest stretch of singletrack this side of the La Sal Mountains with outstanding views of Castle Valley and the Colorado River.

Advance Riders

I don't need to tell you much about biking Moab other than to remind you to stop now and then from your hammering to absorb the beauty of the surroundings. Also, if you have brought your less experienced biking buddies or significant other to Moab, back your pace off so that they will have a more enjoyable experience. Beyond that, start your rides early, bring along and drink large amounts of water and remember to observe proper trail etiquette.

A Brief History

Like the rock formations that dominate the landscape, Moab has enjoyed a colorful and unique history. Indians, Mormon settlers, cowboys, miners, the federal government, movie makers, tourists and mountain bikers have all contributed to the Moab story over the years.

Little evidence remains of the original Native American inhabitants, though the Barrier Canyon people left rare spirit paintings. Later on, the Anasazi and the Fremont People left rock art depicting supernatural beings, clan symbols and countless other writings throughout the valley.

Riding on the Slickrock Bike Trails.

The first white men came to the region in the early 1800s. Trappers and traders traveling on the Old Spanish Trail passed through the Moab Valley to make the relatively safe crossing of the Colorado River.

The Mormons established the Elk Mountain Mission in Spanish Valley in the spring of 1855.

This attempt to settle the Moab Valley, however, was short lived. One version of history (as recounted in Coyote's History of Moab) has the the Mormons run out of the area by Utes. Humiliated by the Mormons, the Utes subsequently attacked and killed several of the men before the mission was abandoned in the fall of 1855.

Meanwhile, Spanish Valley saw the arrival of ranchers, sheepherders, homesteaders, cowboys, and prospectors from various religious affiliations or lack thereof. By 1881, the community variously known as Spanish Valley, Mormon Fort and Grand Valley was named Moab. Some historical references has Moab named from the Bible; but there is speculation that the name may have been influenced by the Paiute word "moapa," meaning "mosquito water," for the swarms of mosquitoes that inhabited the wetlands near town.

Cowboys, sheepherders, and gold miners working claims in the La Sals in the 1890s contributed to making Moab a wild frontier town. One can even speculate that the first bicycles may have been pedaled in Moab during this era as a bicycle craze was sweeping the country at the time.

By the end of the century, the mines had played out. Overgrazing had taken its toll on the Moab environment, so many cattle companies moved north. And sadly, the Native Americans had been displaced and were now confined to reservations. The wild west was not so wild anymore.

In 1906, with the beginning of the conservation movement in the US, the La Sal Mountain Range was added to the nation's system of forest preserves, (now the Manti-La Sal National Forest). This was the beginning of heavy involvement by the U.S. government in the Moab region.

In 1929, Arches National Park was given protection as a National Monument. There ensued for many years a push to preserve much of the scenic lands in the Canyon Country as a national monument. For numerous reasons this did not happen. In 1962, the Glen Canyon Dam was built and completed. A second proposed dam, the Dark Canyon Dam, which was never built, would have flooded much of the region, including the town site of Moab. A remnant of the original proposed national monument became the Canyonlands National Park in 1963. In 1971, Arches National Monument was upgraded to National Park status. In 1972, the Glen Canyon National Recreation Area, contiguous to the west side of Canyonlands, was established.

A colorful aspect of Moab's history that continues to this day is the role of the film industry. Hollywood came to Moab in 1949 after a visit by film director, John Ford, who returned to film Wagonmaster. This was the first of many big screen movies and commercials to be made in the area. Though most movies filmed here have been low budget, there have been some exceptions. Some recent box office successes include

Indiana Jones and the Last Crusade, which features a young Indy in Arches National Park; and *Thelma and Louise*, who cruise through Canyon Country while escaping from the law.

A major boom to Moab in 1952, which also helped save the community from the construction of the proposed Dark Canyon Dam, was the discovery of uranium on the Colorado Plateau. The town prospered, but this was short lived, as the limited market for uranium sent Moab from boom town to bust by the early 1960s. Miners turned their attention to potash, but by 1974, these operations were mechanized and Moab's mining days were all but over. The miner's legacy is the maze of backroads and trails that bikers and 4WD enjoy today.

In the late 1970s, the Bureau of Land Management (BLM) was mandated to perform an inventory of roadless areas for potential wilderness status, which included Negro Bill Canyon and Mill Creek Canyon. The BLM was assaulted by local interests to the point that the BLM deleted them from wilderness consideration. But through the efforts of environmental groups, these areas are now included in wilderness study areas, along with Behind the Rocks, Lost Springs Canyon and Indian Creek.

In 1988, a toxic waste incinerator was proposed to be built along the Colorado River north of Moab, while developers in San Juan County to the south proposed to construct the nation's first high-level nuclear waste dump just outside an entrance to Canyonlands National Park. The projects brought the local population, which included environmentalists, and other activists together, to defeat these projects.

Though in existence for decades, the tourist industry saw a boom in the 1980s. People from around the world were lured to the region by the inspirational beauty of the National Parks. Although couch potato tourists were arriving in droves, there was also a major increase in tourists coming for such participatory sports as river running, backpacking, rock climbing and mountain biking. The actual mountain bike boom was kicked off by mountain bike magazines after the Slickrock Motorcycle Trail was discovered and adopted by early mountain bikers. Within a few years, Moab had become the most famous mountain bike destination in the world.

Though overgrazing and mineral exploration continue as problems in the unprotected areas of Canyon Country, the latest threat to the region's ecosystem comes from us, the tourists. We must all do our part to minimize our individual impact in Canyon Country, and take that philosophy back to our homes.

Among the references I found for this brief look at the history of the area, I especially enjoyed and referred back to *Coyote's History of Moab* (Compost Press, Moab, Utah, 1994) by Jose Knigton. I highly recommend this 60 page booklet that offers a quick read for a unique overview of Moab's history. In addition, *Desert Solitaire*, written by Edward Abbey, while a ranger at Arches in the late 1950s, should be read to expand one's appreciation of the Canyon Country and add to one's environmental consciousness.

What's New

If it has been a few years since your last Moab visit then you will be in for a few surprises. Yes, indeed, this is a boom town.

Moab now has three major bike shops, several new motels and campgrounds and even a McDonalds. The fast food chain claimed to be "Moab's Other Arches," until, in the finest Edward Abbey tradition, repeated monkey-wrenching to the sign eventually convinced the owners to take down the blasphemy.

Perhaps the biggest change for the environmental good is the new camping regulations for several near-by areas and the creation of the toll booth on the Sand Flats Road.

Over the past decade, mountain bikers have been arriving in Moab in ever increasing numbers. One of the most popular areas for camping was along the Sand Flats Road in the vicinity of the Slickrock Trail. What better way to experience Moab than by camping within a short pedal of the most unique mountain bike trail in the world?

Even when the number of visitors was few, this put a strain on the fragile desert environment. As its popularity soared, more and more previously unused areas along the Sand Flats Road were being turned into campsites. Fire rings were sprouting like weeds, people were doing their business behind every rock and shrub, and toilet paper was blowing in the wind.

This began to change in 1994 as the Bureau of Land Management, which oversees the area, instituted a "camping in designated areas only" policy. By cutting the number of Sand Flats sites to 100, they alleviated some of the environmental impact.

There was still the problem of solid waste management. During peak periods, portable toilets were placed along the road. This worked well when they were in place, which unfortunately wasn't often enough. The money to pay for these port-a-pots came from the donations at the Slickrock Trailhead. Unfortunately, the donations did not keep pace with the use. In fact, as user days went up, the donations often went down.

As of March 1995, the BLM has instituted two new policies that will hopefully generate the necessary funds to improve the quality of the Sand Flats Road and Slickrock Trail experience.

The Sand Flats Contact Station is now manned along the Sand Flats Road, between the Lion's Back Campground and the Slickrock Trail. This toll and information booth has started out being open during the day for most of the year, charging a fee from all users. The fees are subject to change, but currently the charge is $1 per person for a three day pass or $10 for an annual pass for individuals on bikes. If you are in a motor vehicle, the charge for a three day pass is $3 for up to two people and $1 for each additional person. In addition to the day use fee, there is also a $4 charge per vehicle per campsite.

The revenue generated from these fees will go toward improvements such as toilet facilities, information kiosk and campsite improvements such as fire rings with grills and picnic tables.

I am sure that some folks will object to the new fees and will attempt to get around the contact station without paying. The reality of the situation is that the fee is reasonable and the money will be going to worthwhile projects that will help preserve the beauty of the area and make your visit more enjoyable.

The Lay of the Land

Moab is situated at 4000 feet elevation in Southeastern Utah in a region commonly referred to as Canyon Country. This is part of the Colorado Plateau that extends into northern Arizona and western Colorado and northwestern New Mexico. In this region you will see sights not found anywhere else in the world. The magnificence of it all is awesome, presented in sandstone, the mineral that gives much of the region's rock its rust color.

The rock layers or strata are like a book that tells the geological story. This story began over 200 hundred million years ago, when the region that was to become the Colorado Plateau experienced numerous cycles of change. The land was alternately above and below sea level for several cycles. After global changes brought lowered sea levels, the plateau dried and became a desert. Then the seas rose again. Eventually, the land was thrust far up above sea level. At this point, the complex drainage that makes up the Colorado River and its many tributaries, cut deeply into the deposits of the plateau to form the incredible and majestic canyons and landforms we see today.

Capturing much of the essence of the desert is Canyonlands and Arches National Parks, both must see areas for Canyon Country visitors. Canyonlands National Park has hundreds of colorful canyons, mesas, buttes, fins, arches and spires. Most notable of the canyons are the two formed by the Green and Colorado Rivers. You can get a permit to bike on specific jeep roads in one of the three districts in the park - Island In The Sky, the Maze and Needles. Better yet, join one of the Moab tour companies for a guided Canyonlands adventure.

The greatest density of arches in the world is in Arches National Park. Erosion sculpted the sandstone, where first narrow sandstone walls or fins were formed, and then crumbled and flaked eventually cutting through the fins, resulting in holes enlarged to arches. Arches can range in height from the minimum three feet to over 100 feet. The arches eventually collapse leaving buttresses. Though there is little off road biking allowed in the park, there are a few open dirt roads.

One last note, the La Sal Mountains, a stone's throw east of Moab rise to almost 13,000 feet above sea level. These mountains provide the spectacular backdrop for most of the mountain bike riding in Canyon Country, and are a cool getaway for summer biking in the area.

This country is so rich and diverse in what nature created that if you even feel a spark of interest in how it has all happened, buy a copy of the *Geology of the Moab Area* by F.A. Barnes (Canyon Country Publications, Moab, Utah, 1993). It provides an excellent read on the regional geology without getting any more technical than necessary, with an easy to follow road log that defines and describes landforms and features mile by mile. This binder sized book is too big to take with you on your bicycle, but as usual you can copy pages for a pedal. Another book by F. A. Barnes, *Canyon Country GEOLOGY* gives a summary of the unique geologic history of the region for the general reader, with a listing of unusual landforms and a section on rock collecting. In addition, Todd Campbell's excellent mountain bike guidebook, *Above and Beyond Slickrock*, provides descriptions of the local geology for each ride.

The Slickrock Trail

For many people, the Slickrock Trail is the essence of the Moab mountain biking experience. All mountain bikers worth their salt need to visit this shrine at some point in their lives.

On several occasions, I have spoken to mountain bikers who made the trip to Moab and only rode the Slickrock Trail. While I think these folks are limiting their exposure to what the region has to offer, I know no visit to Moab is complete without at least spending a few hours following the little white lines on this world renowned trail.

While I am not a fan of off road motorcycles mainly due to the noise factor, I have to hand it to them for the trickle down benefits that mountain bikers have received from the gasoline powered set. I don't even want to think what my body would feel like if it wasn't for the benefits of my 'Rock Shox.'

The Slickrock Trail is another hand me down from these motorized two wheelers. Although you might not guess it from the ratio of mountain to dirt bikes, this trail was originally conceived and developed for motorcycles.

In 1969, Dick Wilson made a proposal to the Bureau of Land Management to create a trials route in the sandstone outcrops east of Moab. The route was plotted and after a study of the possible impact, the trail was given approval in May of that same year.

One of the first tasks of the trail creators was to give it a suitable name. The initial name attached to the project was the Bald Rock Bike Trail. This didn't catch on and other titles including Bare Rock, Hard Rock and Smooth Rock Trail failed to make the final cut. The final solution

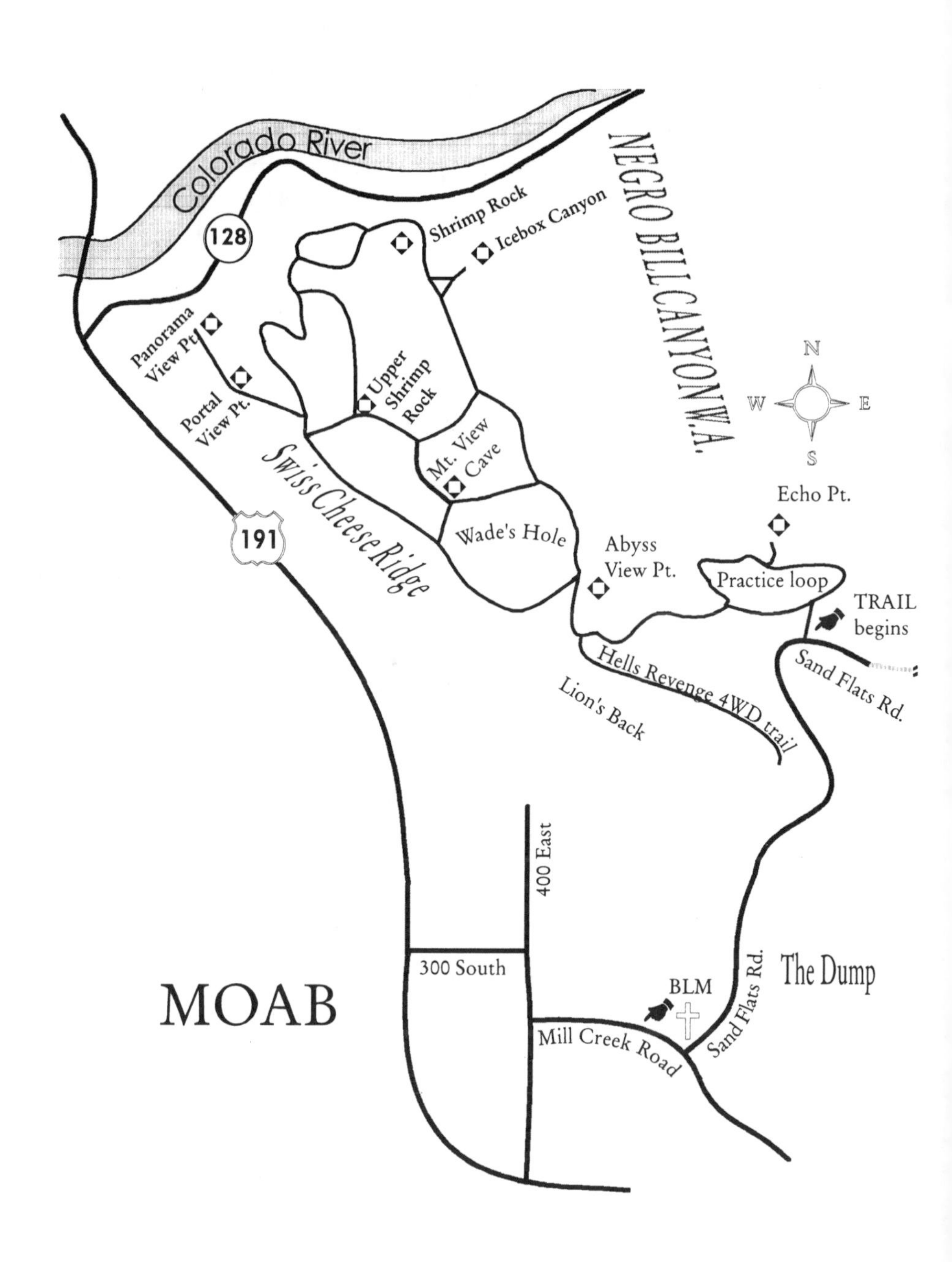

Map: Slickrock Bike Trail

was to name it the Slickrock Trail, which is a common term for much of the local sandstone, although the rough texture of the trail's Navajo sandstone is not necessarily the slick variety.

Dick made the preliminary markings of the main trail and several spurs, some of which have since been allowed to fade away. He also proposed a few names for the now familiar features along the trail such as Abyss View Point and Shrimp Rock. He also attached a few names to places that have not made it into the slickrock riders vernacular.

In June of 1969, BLM workers laid down the white lines that have become synonymous with the trail. The 12-inch template which they used was meant to resemble a knobby motorcycle tread. The trail was officially opened to the public at a dedication ceremony on July 22, 1969.

In 1989, guidebook author Todd Campbell proposed and marked several connecting trails and the Ice Box Spur to increase ride options and to offer possible bail out routes.

The trail never took off in a big way for motorcyclists. The BLM reports that the 1980s saw an average of less than 500 user days per year for the intended riders. However, with the mountain biking boom of the last 10 years, they have seen the explosion of usage by mountain bikers to exceed 100,000 user days per year.

This heavy use on the part of mountain bikers can be considered both an attraction and a detraction of the trail. If you ride this trail during the seasonal peaks, expect to see hundreds of riders. If you are looking for a wilderness experience, forget it. The best way to enjoy the trail with the masses is to consider it a social event. Many bikers tend to gather at the beginning and end of some of the tougher sections of trails. Be social, find out where the other riders are from and make some new friends from around the world. You can also go to school on the other riders lines and techniques. Watch and learn.

If you would like more of a backcountry tour of the trail, consider the following tips. Avoid weekends and the peak weeks around Spring Break and the Fat Tire Festival. If you must ride during these times, begin very early in the day. If you are experienced with the main route, then consider venturing off the beaten path.

For a true wilderness experience, you might want to try the off-season. A few years ago my family stopped in Moab in route to the July Fat Tire Festival in Crested Butte, Colorado. It was so hot during the day that grease was oozing out of the bearings. We laid low during the heat of the day by lounging by the pool and taking a half day float trip on the Colorado. On the fourth of July, we headed up to the Slickrock Trail around 5 PM as the heat of the day was beginning to subside. When we arrived at the parking lot, there were only two other cars. By the time the sun went down, we were alone. The next day we repeated the routine and had the trail to ourselves the entire time.

This contrasted with one of my more recent peak season experiences. We arrived in town a week after Easter figuring that we would miss the spring break crowd. No way. The masses were everywhere. To top it off, we decided to ride the trail on a Saturday. On the plus side, we got a sunrise start and only encountered five or six riders on the first half of the ride. However, as we made our turnaround we began to run into the masses. Nothing, however, prepared us for the shock that was in store for us as we returned to the beginning of the outer loop. At the junction where the outer loop meets back up with the out and back section there were almost 100 riders congregating.

As we headed back on the out and back section we passed several hundred more. At many of the tougher sections, there were scores of riders waiting to take on the difficult lines. This reminded me of the dreaded lift lines in alpine skiing. Take a number please! Fortunately, I sort of expected this so I wasn't bumming. I took the opportunity to talk to many of the other bikers waiting their chance to roll. By the time we made it back to the trailhead, the parking lot was full and the Sand Flats Road was lined with the overflow parking. While I still had a good time, this experience is not one I will repeat.

The Price For Admission

The Slickrock Trail is no longer a free ride. Other than a simple request for donations at the trailhead, biking the Slickrock Trail had been a freebie since its inception. What a deal!

In 1995 this policy has changed as part of the new Sand Flats Recreation Area policy. A toll booth has been established between Moab and the Slickrock Trailhead. The booth will be manned during the day for most of the year. If you are on your bike you will be charged $1 per day or $10 for a yearly pass. If you are in your vehicle, the daily charge is $3 for up to two people and $1 per additional person. This charge is for anyone using the road, not just for Slickrock Trail users. You should also expect to pay if you are riding the Porcupine Rim trail or even sight seeing in your vehicle.

These rates are subject to change, but the plan is to keep them reasonable. As the saying goes, "it would be a bargain at twice the price." The way I look at it is that one buck is a small price to pay for a ride that puts Disneyland to shame. More importantly, the revenue is going toward improvements to the trailhead and along Sand Flats Road.

It Doesn't Have to Be a Black Diamond Ride

All of the mountain bike guidebooks and trail maps give the Slickrock Trail an advanced or black diamond rating. Despite the fact that it is only a little over 12 miles and there are no extended climbs, I would have to agree. On the other hand, the Slickrock Trail should be experienced by everyone, so if you are not an advanced rider, I would not let this rating deter you from tackling at least a portion of this true "classic."

For most beginners and many intermediate riders without a lot of endurance, don't feel like you have to complete the whole ride. You can have just as much fun getting your slickrock skills while biking near the trailhead without committing to the entire length of the circuit. Send your advanced buddies on their way while you work up your skills, confidence and courage.

For you advanced riders, you will love the trail, but don't take it too lightly. If it is your first time, plan on it taking longer than you expect and bring plenty of water. If you insist on dragging along your beginner friends, slow down the pace and give them plenty of time to recover from the tough sections.

So how long does the trail take to ride. Good riders can hammer on through in less than two hours. I personally like to approach it as an all day affair with many breaks and some off the main drag exploring. If you want to make good time, I suggest you ride the trail alone or with one other rider. Once your group gets larger, the laws of social inertia begin to take over and the time to complete the route increases dramatically as you stop at the top of each tough climb to wait for the entire group.

If you do ride in a big group, try to set the pace for the weakest rider. This does not mean waiting for him at the top of each hill and then taking off as soon as he pulls up. If you get impatient with waiting, then use that time to put in some side trail technical practice.

The biggest tip I could pass along would be to get an early start and stay with a casual pace. There shouldn't be any rush as there is so much to see, experience and enjoy.

If you are having a tough time learning the skills necessary to ride the slickrock, then spend some time watching the other riders for some tips on technique. Better yet, see Mark at the World University of Cycling and sign up for one of his "how to ride the slickrock" classes.

The bottom line is that the trail is to be enjoyed and not feared. A good time should and can be had by all. I remember how my 10 year old daughter was in tears the first 15 minutes of her Slickrock Trail experience. However, once she got over her initial fear, she was jamming all over the place with me in pursuit. If she can have a good time on the slickrock, so can you.

It's Easier Than It Appears!

In the summer of 1988, my wife Annie and I were on a Rocky Mountain road trip. On the way to Colorado we stopped off in Moab. Late in the afternoon I took Annie up to get her first experience on the

Finishing the outer loop on the Slickrock Trail.

Slickrock Trail. This was Annie's first year of mountain biking, and two days earlier, she took her first endo while riding in Park City, so she was riding pretty tentatively. In fact, for the first hour or so, she was off her bike more than on.

Slickrock riding can be intimidating. Many riders find themselves on sections that are much steeper than they have ever experienced before and the solid rock surface does not appear to be a friendly environment to crash on.

My encouraging words were not having the usual effect, so I decided to try something different. As the late afternoon shadows were getting longer and longer, I said to Annie. "Gee, you might not want to get off your bike so much, as the sun goes down the rattlesnakes will be coming out." Within seconds, Annie's skills improved dramatically and she was riding whatever came her way.

Negotiating on the Slickrock Trail

Taking a break on the Slickrock Trail

Season to be Mountain Biking

When is the best time to plan your mountain bike vacation to Moab? Good question. Moab can be enjoyed just about any time of the year, but there are certainly times more conducive to mountain biking. It is generally accepted that the ideal seasons for biking Moab are the spring and fall.

You can bike in the winter on most of the lower routes, but the days are short and the temperature can be down right cold. On the plus side, great deals can be had on lodging and you won't find crowds at the trailheads. I can't say from experience what winter biking in Moab is like, but many of the locals enjoy alternating biking days with backcountry skiing in the La Sals.

During the summer, heat is your biggest limiting factor. This is especially true during July and August when daytime high temperatures hover in the 100°F range. If you do show up in Moab in the middle of summer, you will not be alone since many pilgrims take advantage of summer vacation and ride the slickrock, not realizing what they are in for in terms of the temperature.

I wouldn't plan a full on mountain bike vacation to Moab during the summer, but I also wouldn't rule out stopping by for a day or two while enroute to somewhere else. On several occasions, the family and I have stopped in for a short stay while heading to the mountains of Colorado. The key to our enjoyment was riding early and late in the day and spending the time in the middle of the afternoon lounging by the motel pool or floating on the river. Another summer alternative is to head to the hills and spend some time discovering the rides "above" Moab in the La Sal Mountains.

If you are planning a full on Moab adventure, by all means go for the spring or fall. I have always had a preference for the spring as the snow covered La Sal Mountains make for a dramatic backdrop to most of the rides. March can vary from cold to perfect, sometimes in the same trip. My first Moab excursion was in March, and when we arrived in town around midnight, it was snowing. It was so cold on our first ride that we had to wear our full on conditions gear. By the second day, we were able to strip off the wind front tights and by the third, we were in t-shirts and shorts.

April is usually consistently good but also sees the most bikers, May can be perfect to hot and in June you are taking your chances.

I had been coming to Moab for many years before I had a chance to experience the fall. I came, I rode, and I loved it. During September you can hit hot weather, but the longer daylight hours are great. September is also an off-season month as the summer park tourists are gone and the mountain biking hoards have yet to arrive. Plus, if you time it right, you might hit the fall color display in the La Sals.

October is peak mountain bike season. Except for an occasional storm, the weather is usually perfect. On the down side, thousands of other mountain bikers are descending on Moab, with the high tide occurring at the end of the month for the Fat Tire Festival.

If you don't mind the short days, early November can be a real treat since you will have many of the trails to yourself. In addition, the lighting this late in the season can be nothing short of spectacular.

Speaking of crowds, if you are interested in missing the hoards, keep in mind that April and October are especially busy times, especially during Easter break and the week following. I thought I was timing my trip perfectly one spring when we arrived the week after spring break. Wrong. Most of the ski areas in the west close after Easter and hundreds of newly unemployed resort employees head out to Moab to ride, hang out and warm their bones. And in the fall, all of October is busy, especially during the Fat Tire Festival, which is held during the last week of the month.

Average Daytime Temperatures (F)

Jan	Feb	Mar	Apr	May	Jun	Jul	Aug	Sep	Oct	Nov	Dec
49.6	50.4	70.2	72.5	82.4	92.0	99.0	95.3	87.1	73.8	56.0	45.1

Average Monthly Percipitation (inches)

Jan	Feb	Mar	Apr	May	Jun	Jul	Aug	Sep	Oct	Nov	Dec
.53	.62	.71	.79	.57	.45	.49	.87	.83	1.16	.60	.64

As you can see from the chart, Moab generally receives rain every month of the year. Most of the rain comes down rapidly in the form of thunderstorms of short duration.

Getting There Can Be Half The Fun

The majority of the mountain bikers will arrive in Moab in their own car or truck. An occasional biker might make it into town under pedal power and a small minority with more money than time on their hands will manage to fly in. Beyond that, the options are limited. There are few flights available and no existing bus or train service.

Fortunately, driving to Moab does not present much of a problem other than racking up quantities of road miles. I love road trips and believe that with the proper attitude, getting there can be half the fun, although I must admit, that racking up the miles in the back reaches of Nevada can leave something to be desired. However, with an ample supply of good tapes and the anticipation of the biking ahead, I can usually get through the journey with nothing worse than a stiff back.

A good percentage of tourists enroute to Moab travel on Interstate 70 north of Moab and then at Crescent Junction head south for 33 miles. However, if you are arriving on I-70 from the east, I recommend you take the less traveled State Route 128. It saves a few miles but with all the vista points it will probably take a little longer. Route 128 is a windy two lane scenic byway that parallels the Colorado River for much of its length.

Distance in miles, to Moab from some metropolitan areas around the country...

Albuquerque, NM - 335
Chicago, IL - 1410
Denver, CO - 360
Durango, CO - 165
Grand Junction, CO - 115
Las Vegas, NV - 480
Los Angeles, CA - 760
Phoenix, AZ - 470
Salt Lake City, UT - 245
San Francisco, CA - 940

Getting to Moab via air is possible though it certainly is off the beaten flight path, with the only regularly scheduled flights from Salt Lake City. Alpine Air offers three flights daily during the summer months and two per day during the remainder of the year.

Alpine Air's flights are on small nine passenger Cessna's, so don't plan on bringing your bike along. If you take the airborne route you can ship your bike ahead via UPS to Kaibab or Poison Spider Bikes and for a reasonable fee they will build it up and have it ready for you when you arrive.

Although prices are always subject to change, the most current fare quoted for the Salt Lake City to Moab round trip is about *$150* if you make reservations at least eight days in advance. Tickets without advance reservations are about *$225.* (801)575-2839

If you fly into Grand Junction you can charter a flight with Red Tail Aviation, Slickrock Air Guides, or Mountain Flying Service. The charter fare runs about $45 per person with a minimum of three passengers.

Another option is to only fly to Grand Junction, Colorado, which puts you about 115 road miles from Moab. Your best bet from here is to rent a car from Thrifty Car Rental. You can keep the vehicle for the duration of your stay in Moab and then return it to Grand Junction. However, there is a budget alternative. Thrifty's policy allows you to rent in Grand Junction and drop off the car in Moab without an additional charge. At the end of your stay in Moab you can rent a car again to return to Grand Junction. Of course, you will be without a car during your stay, but there are worse places to be without a vehicle. The approximate cost for their least expensive compact car from Grand Junction to Moab is *$40* per day while the return to Grand Junction runs about *$45* per day.

If you have a large group (up to 10 people with bikes) you can hire Eagletree Tours out of Grand Junction to shuttle you to Moab. The cost for this service is *$225.* If you and your buddies are planning on riding the length of Kokopelli's Trail, this service might be a real benefit even if you drive to Moab. The phone number for *Eagletree Tours* is (303)241-4792.

Gearing up for Moab

I am constantly amazed at how unprepared many mountain bikers are before heading into the backcountry. Some just do not know any better. If their biking has been limited to short rides in heavily populated areas, the need to gear up may not have ever presented itself. However, once bikers find themselves heading into a serious backcountry situation, they had better begin to get their act together.

Biking in Moab is certainly no exception. With Moab's combination of desert conditions, a potential for rapid thunderstorms, technical terrain and at times tricky route finding, it can definitely be considered serious backcountry biking. While some rides only require a minimum of gear, heed my advice and head out fully prepared on most of the tours in the area.

There is usually a list of the ten essentials for most backcountry sports. In mountain biking, this list is often longer since you also have to deal with your bike and related accessories.

The following is my list of recommended gear for backcountry biking, followed by a short explanation of some of the items and a section on gearing up for what we refer to as "full on conditions."

Fair weather clothing:

helmet
bike gloves
bike shorts
t-shirt or bike jersey
lightweight Thermax or Capilene top
windbreaker
socks
mountain bike shoes
bandanna or headband

Accessories:

water bottles and Camelback
map and compass
guidebook or trail notes
high energy foods
matches and fire starter
Swiss army knife
sunglasses
toilet paper and zip lock to pack out t-p
sunscreen
lip balm
first aid kit
insect repellent
mini flashlight

camera with extra film and batteries
large capacity fanny pack

Tools:

air pump
tire patch kit
spare tube
tire lever
Allen keys
chain tool
small crescent wrench
Tri-flow
rags
tool bag

At the top of the list is a helmet. I am often amazed that there are still riders out there not wearing them. All I can say is that it is part of the natural selection process. Eventually all stupid bikers that insist on riding without a helmet will be brain dead.

As far as basic bike clothing goes, you probably already have that down from your previous experience. I suggest you use whatever has worked for you in the past. On the other hand, read on if you would like to share some of my biker wisdom.

All I can say about bike shorts, if you haven't come around to bike specific padded shorts, do it now. You will not be sorry. If you have fretted about being seen in public in tight fitting lycra, then you might want to try one of the baggy biking shorts that have been coming into the market in recent years. These alternatives to lycra might not be quite as comfortable for biking, but they do have their plusses. On the other hand, if you wear regular lycra bike shorts, don't worry as you will fit right in along with the hundreds of other lycra clad folks wandering the streets of Moab.

Unless biking early or late season or during a storm front, chances are overheating will be a prime consideration. Loose fitting, light colored shirts are your best bet. If you wear tank-tops, watch out for the inevitable crescent shaped sunburn on your back. My preference is for a t-shirt with the sleeves removed. More and more mountain bikers have started wearing those ugly geek jerseys that you see on the cover of bike magazines. Just remember that the riders pictured are usually paid to wear these abominations. If you insist, try to wear the ones that carry a minimum of advertising.

When the weather is perfect with no chance of thunderstorms, you might be able to get by with just your t-shirt or jersey. However, in just about any backcountry situation, you should be prepared for a change in weather and a possible unplanned night under the stars.

The key to staying comfortable in all weather conditions, from hot to cold is layering. A layering system should include three layers; a wicking layer next to your skin, an insulating layer and, on the outside, wind and/or rain protection.

An important aspect of the layering principle and staying comfortable in the backcountry is to keep tabs on your comfort level and adjust your clothing combinations whenever necessary. If you start sweating, take off a layer. A common mistake that many mountain bikers make is that they don't stop enough to make clothing adjustments. Beginners often think they will be left behind and some riders are too macho to stop. Of course this doesn't apply if you are down to your last layer and are still sweating. Biking naked in the hot desert sun is not a smart idea.

Whether I am hiking, canoeing, backcountry skiing or biking, a lightweight shirt made from Thermax or Capilene or other materials with similar characteristics comes along in my pack. These fast drying materials have the ability to wick the moisture away from your body. Even if you happen to get soaked in a sudden storm, they will still help to keep you warm. Chances are you will not need to use it after the morning chill dissipates for most rides, but when you need it you will be glad you brought it along.

On many fair weather outings when the likelihood of getting lost is minimal, I will forgo the middle insulating layer. However, when there is a good chance of cold or wet weather, I will bring along either a wool sleeveless sweater or an expedition weight Capilene or Thermax top.

Along the same lines, my windbreaker usually stays rolled up at the bottom of my fanny pack, but I still never head out without it. If there is a chance of rain or snow, I will bring along a Gore-tex shell, but most of the time I just pack a very lightweight and breathable windbreaker. I do spray water repellent on the front and shoulders to beef up the rain protection.

As far as tools go, being prepared does not just mean bringing along the right ones, but also knowing how to use them. As long as one person in your party knows how to work on bikes you will probably be OK. However, there is also a great feeling of accomplishment and independence that can be felt if you can handle your own problems. If you totally lack any trailside repair skills, I highly suggest you take a class before leaving home or sign up for one at the World University of Cycling courses when you arrive in Moab.

First and foremost, every mountain biker should know how to fix a flat tire. Other skills can come later, but this one is a must. A few tips concerning flats include. . . .Make sure that there is still glue in your patch kit. Often, glue magically evaporates and you will be left with air. You can even get around this problem now with the glueless patches that have recently hit the market. Also, check to make sure that your pump is working and that it also matches up with the tube type you are using. Most newer pumps can go both ways, schrader and Presta, but many older ones need an adapter.

All riders in your group do not need to have every tool listed. The important thing is that among all of you, every item is covered. There are also many other tools and parts not listed that you might want to bring along, but at some point you have to decide when enough is enough

Heading the accessory list is water. When biking in the desert you want to bring along as much water as you can. Two full bottles are usually a minimum for short rides. For longer rides you should supplement this with a hydration system such as the Camelback which is carried on your back or by packing additional bottles in your fanny pack. I will never bike in Moab again without a Camelback, at least until something better comes along.

To carry all your tools you should use a seat pack. The rest of your gear and clothing should be carried in a fanny pack. I'm not talking about some cheapo fanny that you received for renewing your magazine subscription or opening up a checking account, but rather an honest to goodness quality fanny pack. Many people don't like to carry fanny packs because they have had some bad experiences. I understand this as most fannies ride like a piece of crap when loaded with a few heavy or bulky items. Do yourself a favor and invest in a quality pack like the ones made by Osprey, Cyclesmith, or Dana Designs. I can almost guarantee that it will become one of your favorite articles of gear as you will probably be using it for several of your outdoor pursuits.

The chances are very good that you will have clear weather during most of your Moab visit. However, there is also a fair chance that you will get hit with a storm system. Moab does receive a portion of its annual rainfall every month of the year. If you want to make the most of your stay, you should come prepared for this eventuality.

Some full on conditions gear you should bring to Moab include a Gore-tex or other waterproof jacket, bike tights, heavy wool socks, neck gaiter, wool ear band, wool or synthetic sweater or vest, winter bike gloves and an emergency space blanket. I mention winter bike gloves because that is what most people have. My personal choice is a lightweight glove liner that can fit under my bike gloves along with a waterproof shell. These three pairs are often lighter than a pair of heavy gloves and much more versatile as I can use them in several different combinations.

There is a good chance you will never have the necessity to use this gear on a ride. If nothing else, you might use some of it around camp. On the other hand, it would be a shame to miss an opportunity to experience a desert storm because you left your FOC gear at home.

A few other items you might want to bring on your trip includes an ample supply of rags and perhaps a chain cleaner for after ride clean-up and maintenance. If you do your own bike maintenance, bring along a more elaborate tool kit that will remain at your basecamp. You can bring spare parts such as chains, cables, etc., but I have found that the bike shops prices are about what you would expect to pay at home and they are well stocked. If you are staying in a motel that allows you to bring your bike into your room, you might want to do them a favor and bring an old sheet to park your bike on.

Whether I am camping or moteling, one item I always bring is a comfortable fold-up camp chair. Even when staying in a motel, I occasionally like to drive out of town a short ways, pull out my camp chair, kick back and enjoy the sunset. It sure beats watching TV.

Full On Conditions - I'm Singing in the Rain

A few years back I led a tour to Moab for the outdoor program at California State University at Sacramento. Enroute, we were hit with inclement weather, but my encouraging words to the Moab neophytes aboard the university van was not to worry. We were, after all, I assured them, heading to the desert country.

Well, I can't be right all the time. On the plus side, as we rolled into town, the rain had backed off to a steady drizzle. I made an executive decision and informed the group that we would get motel rooms for the night. I figured I could convince everyone to head out on a "full on conditions" (FOC) ride if we had a warm room and a hot tub to retreat to after the adventure. After settling into our rooms, I used my best motivational techniques and before long we were all geared up for a "FOC" ride.

I theorized that Hurrah Pass would be a good choice since the road surface is not one to "mud up" and the mostly uphill route to the pass would make for a swift retreat if necessary. We began under a light drizzle that soon let up. The casual climb warmed us up and we began stripping off the gear. We were completely surrounded by ominous dark skies that were tightening around us like a noose. Before we were even halfway into the final approach the rains returned. Ken, the roadie, expressed his doubts about continuing on, but when I informed him that a few of the gals were off the front he changed his mind and continued on. Drizzle, drizzle, pour, pour. The rain let up as we crested out at the pass. Everyone agreed that this was well worth the effort since the view, which is always great from Hurrah Pass, was especially dramatic under the stormy skies.

We talked about continuing on, but as we observed the weather play out it became apparent that it was destined to get more intense. We made what turned out to be a good call of retreat and began the descent. Within minutes, all hell broke loose as the rain picked up in intensity. The canyon walls began weeping - brown creeks everywhere. We were relatively warm, but the lightning was a definite concern. I loved the way it added an audio dimension to the surreal landscape but we could have done without the element of danger. I could hear the sound bite - "Biker fried on Hurrah Pass, film at 11."

Despite the deluge, attitudes were great. No whining was rearing its ugly head. Just before the only climb on the return, the monsoon began. It was raining cowboys and Indians. Flash flood warnings went off in the back recesses of my brain. The lightning was way too close for comfort as we rode in the proverbial eye of the storm. The sights were mind blowing. Crystal clear waterfalls appeared at every gap along the slickrock canyon walls and plummeted almost a thou-

sand feet in a shimmering free fall. The rains gave the rock walls a glaze that from a distance had the appearance of ice or snow. To top it off, Willy Wonka chocolate rivers gushed down every ravine and gully, sometimes turning the road into a river channel. Great stuff, those chocolate waterfalls. Man, I was grooving to the max - big time. I frequently stopped to O-wow the situation and soak in the sights. A turn of my head, and the water would pour off my helmet and down my back. Chilly.

The rain picked up in intensity as we neared the crux of the tour, the last exposed ridge before the final descent. We hugged the wall and stayed low - we didn't want anyone to fry as we rode along with the crome-moly lightening rods under our butts. I peaked out with biker euphoria by the time we hit the pass. The rains let up and the lightening rambled on to the east. We were safe enough to literally drink in the view. In fact, we almost drowned in it.

From here, the final retreat was fast as we biked through streams of liquid sand. I did stop several times to look around and laugh out loud. So much fun! I hoped that everyone was having at least half the fun that I was. Heck, I knew I would be happy if they were having fun period. I didn't want a revolt 900 miles from home. What a groove! Despite being soaked to the bone, I could have spent another hour or two watching nature's awesome display. But alas, there was a job to be done so I continued on, the last to reach the van.

I imagine that if you asked the participants on the tour, which ride was the most awlsome, they would probably mention the sunny days on the Slickrock Trail or Poison Spider Mesa.

For this slightly off-beat biker, the FOC tour to Hurrah Pass has gone down as a top 10 ride of all time. No singletrack, not a technical jeep trail, or the smartest thing to be riding under a lightning storm on top of metal frame bikes, but it did feature an unforgettable, awesome, display of nature's power and beauty!

Heading to Hurrah Pass in full on conditions

Trail Etiquette

Mountain biking has over the years suffered with a less than positive image as a sport primarily for testosterone charged maniacs speeding blindly down trails, wrecking havoc with anyone or anything that happens to be in their way. While I must admit, there are a few mountain bikers that fit this description, this stereotype is not the norm.

Wherever mountain bikers go, they must be aware that they are ambassadors for the sport and must ride in a safe and responsible manner. In many parts of the country, land access is being limited to mountain bikers due to real or imagined problems resulting from their use or misuse.

Despite being one of the most popular forms of recreation in Moab, mountain bikes still have their local critics and it is important that a mountain bike code of ethics be followed, not only to maintain our image and keep the trail open to us, but most importantly, to protect the fragile desert environment

Several organizations such as the International Mountain Bike Association (IMBA) and the National Off-Road Bicycle Association (NORBA) and individuals (such as guidebook authors) have printed various versions of a mountain biker's code. The following is a list of backcountry rules that all bikers should adhere to at all times.

* Bike on open trails only. In the Moab area, this includes staying off all hiking trails in the National Parks.
* Leave no trace. Minimum impact biking should be your goal. Stay on the trail. Do not cut switchbacks or attempt to bike around obstacles on the trail. In reality, most of the routes in Moab are on jeep roads and not singletrack, but the rule still applies. Do not litter, and better yet take this a step beyond and pick up any litter that you come across, within reason, of course. As the modified version of the old adage goes, "take nothing but pictures and leave nothing but bike tracks.

Friendly chit-chat, trading a little mud on Sand Flats Road.

* Always bike under control. There are times to go fast, but there are also times to keep your speed down. Especially slow down for blind turns. The rule of thumb is to maintain a speed so that you can stop within your line of sight.
* Yield to other trail users. Always yield to hikers and bikers. If you encounter other bikers, the rider heading uphill has the right of way. Give motor vehicles ample room to pass and if you pass them make sure that they know you are there.
* Do not spook livestock.
* Always leave cattle gates as you find them.
* Respect private property
* Be prepared! Before heading into the backcountry riders should be both physically and mentally prepared. This means not only carrying the appropriate gear for the conditions, but also bringing along some common sense and the proper attitude.

Special Moab and Desert Etiquette

Do not ride or walk over cryptogamic soil. Cryptogamic soil is often referred to as the top soil of the desert. Made up of a combination of lichens, fungus, moss and bacteria, this living organism literally holds the desert in place by preventing or slowing down the erosion of soil due to wind and rain. It also serves an important function by assisting in the development of nutrients for the desert ecosystem. The soil is identified by its dusty black color and its rough texture. (All three major bike shops in Moab have displays of cryptogamic soil.) It is also easily damaged by footprints or tire tracks. One biker can do enough damage to this slow growing organism that it could take a century or more to recover.

One aspect of Moab riding off trail contrary to the general rule of staying on the trail is slickrock riding. On many of the large slickrock playgrounds you will be able to make your own way, limited only by your ability and imagination. However, if there is a gap in the slickrock, be very careful when portaging that you do not disturb any of the cryptogamic soil. This is the exception to the "take only pictures and leave only bike tracks" theory. Hop rocks wherever possible and back off and search for another route if a "**no** impact" path can not be found.

* After a rainfall, depressions in the slickrock create pockets of water. These potholes are another important aspect of the desert eco-system. The obvious role is as a supply of water for the animals of the desert. However, they are also the home for many forms of aquatic life, many of which lie dormant when the holes are dry. Do not bike through or even make contact with the water. Any contaminants can cause irreversible damage.
* Do not disturb historical artifacts. Preserve these treasures for others to admire.

The desert is a quiet place - keep it that way. Sound travels well in canyon country. An occasional spontaneous shout of glee is perfectly understandable and perhaps acceptable. On the other hand, constant hooting and hollering in the backcountry takes away from not only your experience, but that of everyone within earshot. This also holds true in camp. Loud music certainly has its place, but it should not be part of the desert camping experience. Bring your Walkman if you want to rock.

We had been biking all day on a weekend in the Monitor and Merrimac area and we had not heard or seen a soul. This was especially appealing since the day before we had shared the Slickrock Trail with several hundred other fat tire flyers.

The M&M ride was quite a contrast to the technically demanding slickrock. Other than the occasional sand pit, it was easy going. After looping the Monitor and Merrimac Buttes we spent some time napping at the Determination Towers. To say we were having a casual day would have been an understatement. Although this tour would bore many riders, I was having a wonderful time enjoying the desert solitude.

On our return, we decided to take an alternate route to Courthouse Wash. While rounding an unnamed butte, we came across the only other bikers we were to see all day. They were friendly enough and we exchanged hellos. We were also heading in the same direction. Bummer. These idiots must have thought we were at an amusement park as they proceeded to scream at the top of their lungs for the next hour. Even when we veered off and were over a mile away we still had to deal with their presence. Bummer.

Trailside repairs are part of the whole experience.

Bike Shops

On my first visit to Moab in 1988, Rim Cyclery was the only bike shop in town. It was actually a required part of the Moab mountain bike experience to stop by Rim Cyclery for a look, spend a few dollars on your bike or on mountain bike related souvenirs. Now there are three full-on shops to choose from, as well as a few other operations where you can take your bike in for repairs, or to rent a good quality mountain bike. No biker's vacation to Moab is complete without a visit to each of the three primary shops.

Competition has brought out the best in all the shops and excellent service seems to be the status quo in town. All the shops realize that visitors want to make the most of their vacation time,and having to leave your bike at the one of the shops for a few days awaiting for repairs is unheard of, in this biker's town. Most shops also open by 8:00 am and close late. The goal of every shop is rapid turnaround on repairs with the vast majority of work done while you wait. When you consider that this is a tourist destination, prices for parts and repairs for the most part are very reasonable.

Kaibab Touring Center
391 South Main Street - (800) 451-1133 (801) 259-7423

A few years back, the good folks at Kaibab Mountain Bike Tours saw a need for another bike shop in Moab to service the legions of visitors descending on their town, and also as a way to support their mountain bike tour operation. In their short history, they have developed an excellent reputation for service, sales and rentals.

One aspect that Kaibab is really proud of is their experienced staff. The Kaibab employees are all serious mountain bikers that really do ride and know first hand what the region has to offer. Guide books are great, but it is even better to get a personal opinion on what would be a good ride for a particular group or time of the year.

The Kaibab Touring Center may be the smallest full service shop in town, but this converted gas station next to City Market is well stocked

Kaibab Bike Shop

and always hopping. Perhaps, because of the lack of space, Kaibab does not feature a full line of production bikes. Instead, they choose to focus on a fine collection of framesets from Salsa, Bontrager, Slingshot, Turner, and Ibis. They also carry a full line of clothing as well as just about any accessory you might imagine.

I can say first hand that their service is top notch. They always have several mechanics on duty with instant turnaround as their their goal. Every time that I or one of my companions brought our bikes in, we were taken care of before we were able to finish browsing around the store, and the repair rates were downright cheap.

Kaibab also has a stable of 50 rental bikes with front suspension. The basic rate is *$22* per day or *$35* for demo bikes which include some fully suspended models. A special service they provide is assembling your bike when it is shipped via UPS to them. When you arrive in town, your bike will be rebuilt and waiting for you. When you are ready to leave town, they will box up your bike and ship it home for you.

Poison Spider Bikeshop

Poison Spider Bicycles
497 N. Main St. - (800) 635-1792 or (801) 259-7882

Poison Spider Bicycles is another bike shop that was started as a way to service a tour company, in this case, Nichols Expeditions. It has since evolved into a full service bike and outdoor shop that can stand on its own merits.

My first experience at Poison Spider was in their old shoebox sized shop, which featured a helpful staff, a minimum of inventory, good service but barely enough room to move around. This isn't the case anymore as they have recently stepped up several notches with the completion of their beautiful new building at the same location.

Poison Spider, like Kaibab is owned and operated by mountain bike enthusiasts who are always willing to share their expertise and assist you in getting the most out of your Moab experience.

Just because they have gotten bigger does not mean that they are not still committed to service to their customers. With their expanded service area they have increased their ability to maintain a one day or sooner bike turnaround. Their work is thorough and the prices are fair.

Poison Spider doesn't just sell and service bikes; it is a full on outdoor shop with camping equipment, climbing gear and even coin operated showers out back. They carry a full line-up of bikes from Diamond Back, Marin, Cannondale, Manitou and Yeti with a complete selection of bike accessories and clothing. They also have an 80 bike rental fleet ranging from rigid fork bikes for *$22* to fully suspended Cannondales for *$40* per-day. They also have a full complement of camping gear rentals featuring equipment from Sierra Designs.

Rim Cyclery Bikeshop

Rim Cyclery
94 West 100 North (801) 259-5333

You have to hand it to Robin and Bill Groff for their forsight. Despite personally not being mountain bikers, they recognized the need for a bike shop in Moab and Rim Cyclery was born. It wasn't long before *'Rim'* became a shrine for all biker pilgrims to visit during their visit. The shop prospered and the owners of this monopoly jokingly called themselves Robem and Billem as they made a small fortune from the bikingboom.

Rim is not as popular with mountain bikers as it once was because it lacks the "run by and for" mountain bikers attitude prevalent at Kiabab and

Poison Spider Bicycles. It is perhaps the only shop in town where you might see some of the staff on a smoke break. On the other hand, I have always found the bike mechanics to be very knowledgeable and friendly. I suggest you go straight to the shop if you have any technical questions.

Despite not having the best reputation with experienced bikers, they still do a great business in bike and outdoor gear sales and repair and are certainly worth of your patronage, if for nothing else than a cup of coffee from the expresso cart that is set up outside.

Rim's current stable of bikes for sale includes Specialized, GT, Klein, Merlin, American, Dean, Ibis and Mountain Goat.

World University of Cycling

World University of Cycling
606 South Main - (801) 259-8258

When is a bike shop not a bike shop? The answer is when it is the World University of Cycling. Eccentric mountain biker Marc Horwitz's "non-shop" on the south end of town has some semblance to a traditional bike shop - there is a repair area, rentals and some basic essentials for sales such as tubes, patch kits, water bottles, and maps, but that is where the similarities end. The main focus at the World University of Cycling is fun and education.

According to Marc, the most important item he has to offer is information. Drop on by and Marc will give you an ear full of biker wisdom and Moab tips. In-house classes include trailside maintenance and repair and backcountry biking basics. One of his favorite classes that he offers in the field is an introduction to biking the slickrock. Marc sees many riders, both beginners and more experienced, thrashing on the Slickrock Trail. His slickrock class is geared to having you master the intricacies of biking on this unique terrain.

The World University of Cycling also distinguishes itself as the smallest shop in town but with the largest expresso cart. In this case, the cart is a full-on diner, also owned by Marc, that shares the same building as his bike business. The Spoon and Tune gives you the opportunity to eat a great meal while your bike is getting a free safety inspection.

The World University of Cycling is definitely worth a visit, if for nothing else than to hear Marc espouse the spirit of mountain biking, as he sees it.

Western Spirit Cycling
38 South 100 West (800) 845-BIKE (801) 259-8732

As part of their touring operation, Western Spirit Cycling has a small rental and repair facility at their headquarters. I have yet to deal with them but they claim most repairs are made while you wait. They also have a great fleet of top quality rentals including a tandem model.

Mountain Bike Tour Companies

Discovering the wonders of the Moab backcountry on your own is easily done, but if you are interested in having the locals show you around, there is no shortage of experienced mountain bike guide services. Offerings range from half day tours out of Moab to week long backcountry affairs exploring many of the outstanding routes in Canyonlands National Park, the La Sals mountains and other neighboring areas.

Some people have the opinion that guided tours are just for the inexperienced. I wholeheartedly disagree. Anyone, no matter how experienced, can enjoy tours offered by these fine outfitters. I consider myself a very experienced mountain biker. I research and write mountain bike guidebooks, and run my own guide service in the Lake Tahoe region. So what do I do for vacation? Well, at least once a year, I take a trip with another tour operation. Like wow, man, this is a real vacation.

Some of the benefits of using a guide-service include delicious food prepared by someone else while you kick back, vehicle support, route finding, and going to and learning more about an area from knowledgeable person.

Of course, money can be the limiting factor preventing many people from using one of these companies. If you can afford it, you will not regret it.

Touring with Kaibab Mountain

Kaibab Mountain/Desert Bike Tours
391 South Main Street
(800) 451-1133, (801) 259-7423, Fax (801) 259-6135

My wife Annie and I have taken a couple of the multi-day tours from those offered by the good folks at Kaibab and between us we award them four thumbs up. Yep, these are the same folks that run my favorite bike shop next to the City Market.

So what do we like about Kaibab? Like most tour companies that have been around awhile (since 1987), they have their act together. The tours are well organized and run very smoothly. Kaibab's attitude runs from the top to the bottom of their operation - they love to have fun with mountain bikes and it shows. Owners Brett Taylor and Jessica Stabrylla and their staff are friendly, accommodating and do not attempt to come off as bike gods.

Current multi-day Moab offerings during the spring and fall include the White Rim Trail, the Maze, and Lockhart Basin. During the summer months they escape the heat with their Sierra La Sal and Trail of the Ancients tours. They also offer a combination tour that includes mountain biking in the Maze or La Sal mountains with whitewater rafting down Cataract Canyon. In addition, Kaibab offers a limited number of "Women's" tours each year.

Kaibab also leads custom day and half day tours out of their bike shop. Groups of six or more can enjoy guided "days of descent". These routes range from the Shafer Trail to Potash, which includes a brief stint on the White Rim Trail and spectacular views below Dead Horse Point, a descent from Polar Mesa down to the Colorado River following a beautiful section of Kokopelli's trail, and the half day Gemini Bridges shuttle tour. To avoid the summer heat, they will also take you to over 10,000 feet to Geyser Pass in the La Sal mountains to begin a 6,000+ foot descent back to Moab. Many of Kaibab's guides are also available for hire on any number of local tours.

The Kaibab guides are always on the lookout for other tour possibilities in the Moab area and far beyond. They currently run summer tours in the Kaibab Plateau along the North Rim of the Grand Canyon and winter tours in Belize.

In conjunction with their bike shop, Kaibab has the ability to supply bicycle rentals as well as camping gear such as tents, sleeping bags and pads. If you are traveling from afar and do not want to deal with the hassle of transporting your bike with you, you can ship your bike ahead to the shop and it will be reassembled and waiting when you arrive in town.

Rim Tours
94 West, 100 North
(800) 626-7335 - 259-5223

Another fine outfit is Rim Tours. Kirstin Peterson and Matt Hebberd founded the original mountain bike tour company in Moab and have been refining their skills since 1985. Rim Tours has done an outstanding job building a great reputation with their Moab tours as well as an interesting selection of offerings in the mountains of Colorado. I have talked to several mountain bikers that have joined Rim for a backcountry adventure and they had nothing but praise for this outfit.

Although Rim Tours does not operate their own bike shop, they have recently added their own fleet of rental bikes to go along with their camping rentals (sleeping bags, pads and tents). They are also loosely affiliated with Rim Cyclery, which gives them access to a bike shop to better serve the needs of their guests.

Rim has a full slate of Moab offerings which include the White Rim Trail, a Moab Bed and Breakfast with lodging at the Sunflower Hill or Canyon Country B&Bs, the Maze, Needles to Moab, Tour of the La Sals, and a fall La Sal Foliage Tour. A unique Rim tour that sounds very enticing is their six day 200 mile Telluride to Moab route that gives participants an opportunity to experience many contrasting environments.

Rim also offers day and half day tours every Wednesday and Saturday or when a group of three or more is interested in a guided Moab classic such as Gemini or the La Sal descent.

In addition to Moab area rides, Rim is also one of the most experienced Colorado tour companies. Included in their Colorado offerings are an advanced Crested Butte singletrack adventure, a mellower Crested Butte Inn Tour, The Colorado Trail Tour that covers some of the best continuous single track there is along a portion of the Colorado Trail, a tour of the high country in the San Juan mountains and a Grand Mesa excursion out of Grand Junction.

Matt and Kirstin are currently working on new tours including the South Rim of the Grand Canyon, Costa Rica and even a high country adventure in Nepal.

Western Spirit Cycling
38 South 100 West
(800) 845-BIKE , (801) 259-8732

Western Spirit is another top notch tour company. The company began running tours in 1990 and is owned and operated by local mountain bike legend Lu Warner. Often referred to as Crazy Lu, he currently holds the White Rim Trail record of approximately seven hours and eleven minutes. Why anyone would want to do this is beyond me, but that is why he is called Crazy Lu. Anyway, I digress.

Western Spirit offers a full gambit of Moab multi-day adventures including every mountain biker's standard, the White Rim Trail. However, they also run a unique surf and turf version of this classic tour. The seven day sea kayak and mountain bike combo starts as a three day flatwater paddle down the Green River. On the fourth morning, guests trade in their boats for bikes and finish out the trip on the White Rim Trail.

Other Moab adventures include The Trail of the Ancients, a Moab Inn tour complete with lodging at the comfortable Mayor's B&B, three days of the Best of Moab riding, the Maze, and a five day jaunt on Kokopelli's Trail.

Although day tours are not a regular offering of Western Spirit, they can be arranged by special request for groups of four or more. WS also rents mountain bikes and can perform bike repair from their Moab headquarters.

Western Spirit has also built up quite a good reputation with their tours up and down the Rocky Mountains. Current offerings include Telluride to Moab, Colorado Singletrack near Durango, the North Rim of the Grand Canyon and a plethora of tours in the Sun Valley region of Idaho. Their backcountry hot springs tour in Idaho is calling my name.

Always looking for great places to ride in the off-season, Lu has recently added a New Zealand adventure. This 10 day affair features unique biking in the Hauraki Gulf of the North Island including four days exploring the Great Barrier Island, known for its white sand beaches and spectacular coastline.

Nichols Expeditions
497 North Main St. - (800) 635-1792 (801)259-7882

Unlike Kaibab, Rim and Western Spirit, Nichols Expeditions does not just mainly focus on mountain bike tours, but offers a range of adventures from sea kayaking, whitewater rafting and backcountry skiing. Although I couldn't peg down exactly when they began mountain bike tours, owners Chuck and Judy Nichols have been leading wilderness travel adventures since 1978.

Chuck and Judy also own Poison Spider Bicycles and the headquarters of their tour company is located upstairs at the greatly expanded new digs on Main Street.

Nichols Expedition's Moab offerings include the White Rim Trail, The Maze and the Needles. One feature you might notice about Nichols tours is that they tend to be a day longer for similar trips offered by other companies. Their theory is that the relaxed pace makes it more comfortable for less experienced riders. Hikes and explorations are included to give everyone the opportunity to become more intimate with the surroundings.

They currently do not offer any regular day tours from Moab, but they have recently added a "Newcomers" clinic. These "on-the-bike" classes can be geared for any ability level and will help newcomers to Moab adapt and learn to ride the rugged conditions of the local roads and trails.

Other mountain bike tours offered include the North Rim of the Grand Canyon and an Idaho Hot Springs adventure.

From their full service bike shop they offer bike and equipment rentals, repair service and shipping and receiving (along with assembly and disassembly) of bikes.

Miscellaneous Offerings

The San Juan Hut Systems
117 North Willow Street
Telluride, Colorado 81435 (303)728-6935

Although not a Moab company, San Juan Hut Systems offers a unique way to experience the mountains of Colorado and the desert of southeastern Utah. Utilizing their system of well stocked backcountry huts, participants can ride the 205 miles from Telluride to Moab on a self guided basis. The huts are stocked with food and sleeping bags and riders need only carry their clothing and other personal items.

Dial Two Five Nine-Taxi Shuttle
21 Williams Trailer Ct - (801) 259-8294

Only in Moab will you see bike racks on a taxi. Two Five Nine-Taxi provides a shuttle service for mountain bikers to the various trailheads around town. If you would like to ride *Porcupine Rim* without the 2000 foot grunt from town but you don't want to mess with setting up a shuttle, then call 259-taxi. Other common shuttles include *Gemini Bridges*, the top of the *Shafer Trail* and the *La Sals*.

Guidebooks

On my first visit to Moab, pickings were slim for guidebooks and maps. As far as I know, Todd Campbell's ***Beyond Slickrock: Rides to Nowhere***, was the only one in existence. At least that was all my friends and I could find.

Todd did help us to find a few great rides and managed to assist us in getting lost at least once. This little pocketbook published in 1987, featured twelve rides that have withstood the test of time. If the descriptions were at times hard to follow, at least the maps were pretty good, and we appreciated using the fruits of Todd's labor.

If you see this book today, I do not recommend purchasing it, unless you are like me and enjoy collecting older mountain bike guidebooks .

The second mountain bike specific guide that I came across was ***Canyon Country Mountain Biking*** by F.A. Barnes and Tom Kuehne published in 1988. Barnes is a prolific author in Canyon Country with guidebooks and informative texts covering hiking, geology, camping, highway touring, history, and off highway vehicle travel.

I used this book on a couple visits and found it easier to use than *Beyond Slickrock.*

The narrative is good and most of the maps are usable, although some are almost useless. *Canyon Country Mountain Biking* is also accompanied by some decent photographs that give you a visual perspective of what you are in for. A real bargain for its $8 cover price.

√ ***Above and Beyond Slickrock*** (A&BS) is Todd Campbell's second attempt at sharing his labor and love with the rest of us and he did us all a great favor. Every group of mountain bikers that heads into Moab should have a copy in their possession. I highly recommend *Above and Beyond Slickrock, $16.95.*

The original book was a 70 page pamphlet of sorts, this version is a handful. That fact is perhaps its only drawback. I haven't put the book on a scale, but it is a hefty son of a gun and because of this most copies will not make to the trails. Users of this heavy volume are left with the choice of memorizing the route, making a few handwritten notes or copying the pages containing the information needed to take on the trail.

In any event, Todd's descriptions are significantly improved over his original work, the maps are very good and his black and white photography is almost worth the price of the book. I suggest you read this book in its entirety before you head to Moab. Besides the great route descriptions, you can learn about the local geology, natural history, backcountry etiquette, and desert biking tips. Once you have finished reading it, choose the routes you will more than likely ride and make copies of the appropriate pages at your local copy shop. Don't forget to bring the book along to Moab, however, as you might end up trying a ride or two that wasn't in your pre-trip plans.

√ If you're planning to do your biking in the Moab area, I would suggest that you stick with Todd's book. However, if you would like to sample some of the outstanding biking opportunities in other parts of Utah, I recommend *"Mountain Biker's Guide to Utah"* by Gregg Bromka instead. This guide is one of a series published by Menasha Ridge and Falcon Press called *"America by Mountain Bike Series."*

The quality of the guides in the series varies widely from book to book, depending on their authors, but in my opinion, Gregg is the best of the bunch. Although only 20 of the 80 rides in this guidebooks are in the Moab region, it is still more than enough to satisfy the casual Moab visitor. Not only did Gregg made an excellent tours selection, but his descriptions are very detailed, accurate and easy to follow.

This three hundred plus pages, several pounds guide is a good reference, but not to be taken along in the backcountry. The cost of this book is *$14.95.*

Bicycle Utah has published a series of Utah guide pamphlets and included in the series is one that covers the Canyonlands region. This little *$6* book has twenty rides in the Moab region, three of which are actually road rides (boo, hiss). This guide is pretty usable as its size encourages you to pack it along.

On my last visit to Moab I picked up a copy of the latest edition to the menagerie of local guidebooks. When I first spotted ***Moab or Bust*** by Brad and Tam (that is right, no last names are listed), I thought this might be the perfect pocket companion for first time visitors to Moab. This handy, dandy lightweight pamphlet weights less than a half eaten PowerBar and features eight of the most popular rides, many of which are considered "must do" classics. All this for only *$4.50.*

Upon closer examination, I have my doubts. I do not have a problem with the lack of editing, which just adds to the funkiness of the book. On the other hand, I have ridden seven of the eight tours and I am not sure I would have been able to follow their trail descriptions on several of them. This is especially true on the Porcupine Rim Trail. On others, the all too brief descriptions leave out much of the great side routes that Todd Campbell has steered me to. For instance, on the Amasa Back Trail, Todd points out a side spur that leads to an outstanding vista point above the Colorado River. I spent hours soaking up the wonderful vibes from this spot. Had I been following along with *Moab or Bust*, I might have missed it altogether.

Brad and Tam also say on the cover "eight great rides from easy to . . . ." That is good so far, but once you get inside the book, there is no mention of difficulty ratings or how much climbing is involved; and on only two of the rides is the mileage even mentioned.

Well, I am not going to rag any more on this book because I like the concept so much. Hopefully, before the next printing, Brad and Tam will go back to the drawing board and take care of at least some if not all of the glitches. With just a little more information and attention to detail, this could become another "must have" item for the Moab traveler.

Another book I purchased on my last trip but I have yet to use is ***Kokopelli's Trail*** by Peggy Utesch. This is another of the books by F.A Barnes' Canyon Country Publications. Despite not having used this book in the field, it appears to be a good choice for bikers interested in tackling all or part of the 130 mile route between Loma, Colorado and Moab. The book has many features in its favor, one of which is its bargain price of $5. In addition, Peggy does a fine job with the trail descriptions, the maps are more than adequate and there are many photographs.

Peggy Utesch and her husband Bob have another fine guidebook titled ***Mountain Biking in the Canyon Rims Recreation Area.*** The CRRA is located south of Moab on the western and southern borders of Canyonlands National Park. Although not nearly as well known or as heavily used as the National Park lands or the mountain biking trails closer to Moab, it is still a spectacular region with many excellent mountain biking routes. If more people will follow Peggy and Bob's lead and bike in the CRRA it will help to help to alleviate some of the pressure on other Moab bike areas. Just like Peggy's Kokopelli's Trail book, I give this a thumbs up as it is well written, easy to follow, and a bargain to boot at only $5. Both guides are also an ideal size and weight for field use. One drawback is that it does not include maps, but in reality, one should carry the appropriate topo map or the ***Off-Road Vehicle Trial Map for the Canyon Rims Recreation Area***.

Between the rock and heaven.

Video Guide

Bike Adventures In Moab by Wayfinders, Inc. is a unique approach to the traditional guidebook. What Wayfinders has created is a visual guidebook. After covering the basics of what to bring on a desert tour, they provide highlights of 20 mountain bike tours. The beginning of each ride has a section covering distance, elevation gain, difficulty level and directions to the trailhead. From there, they follow a few bikers as they tour the highlights of each trail.

You must understand that this video is definitely not a substitute for a good guidebook and topo maps, but it isn't really meant to be. Not too many bikers are going to be carting a battery powered video player and monitor on their bikes so they can see whether the trail forks right or left. Instead, the video is meant to inspire and to give viewers a taste of what the region has to offer. If you were planning a trip to Moab and you needed some fellow travelers, I suggest you invite some prospects over, show them the video and begin making plans. At *$19.95*, it is more than I would care to pay since the money would be better spent on Todd's book, but, if you can find a copy for rent at one of your local bike shops, do so.

My only complaint besides the hookey sound track, is the editing was done to make the riders look flawless and not show any dabs. As soon as the riders are about to dab, endo or bail throughout the video, they cut away. Hey guys, it is not a crime to crash.

Moab Mountain Bike Maps

I love maps. At home I have a huge collection of maps covering places where I have been or hope to visit in the future. I always try to procure a selection of maps to a region before going there so I will have a better understanding of the area. If you are traveling to Moab, you are fortunate in that there is a multitude of maps from which to choose. They range from the very detailed *United States Geological Survey 7.5 minute* topographicals to mountain bike specific maps that cover the entire Moab region.

Maps are considered one of the essentials that should be carried when on a backcountry mountain bike ride. Unless you are biking the very well marked Slickrock Trail or riding with someone that knows the trail well, you should carry some kind of map with you.

The area that is often described as the Moab region encompasses a huge tract of land surrounding the town. Many fine maps are available that fulfill different needs. You need to decide whether you want maximum detail or perhaps one map that does it all. Is the map itself good enough for your needs, or do you want something that also has special information geared toward the mountain biker? The following is a rundown on the various maps I have found for the Moab region. This should help you find the map or combination of maps best for you.

My first choice for Moab mountain bike maps are the Moab East and **Moab West** publications from Latitude 40°, Inc. I consider these two maps an essential piece of Moab equipment. Between the two maps, you will have a great overview of the vast majority, if not all, the Moab rides, including the La Sal Mountains. The scale is smaller than I would like (1:75,000 which translates into 1 inch = 1.2 miles), there is so much good information on these maps that you could almost do without a guidebook. (If I had to choose between a guidebook and these maps, I would prefer the maps.) In fact, on the back of the maps are detailed trail descriptions mostly written by Todd Campbell, the author of *Above and Beyond Slickrock*. These are not only maps, but works of art, printed in waterproof paper. The revised second editions were released in October of 1994. The price for these outstanding maps is $8-9 each. You may come across a few copies priced for around $5. These were printed on paper that is not water or tearproof and this less expensive version has been discontinued. If you are given the option between the two, I would suggest that you fork out the extra bucks. Go with the more durable versions.

If true route finding is what you are into, then the best maps to supplement the above are the ***United States Geological Survey 7.5 minute topographical maps***. These are the most detailed maps of the region with a scale of 1:24,000 (one inch equals about two fifths of a mile). The greater detail that these maps provide will enable you to more easily visualize the terrain. On the down side, 54 of these maps are needed to cover the area depicted on the two Latitude 40° maps. At *$3.50* a pop, that comes to *$189.* Another drawback is that these maps lack information devoted to mountain bikers that is found on some of the specialty maps. It is a good idea to purchase the few selected USGS maps that cover the tours you plan to ride. Even if you are sure of your route. If you should ever get lost, you will have a much better chance of pinpointing your location with the appropriate USGS-topo.

Trails Illustrated offers a few maps that might be of interest to mountain bikers. The first one is ***Moab Area Mountain Bike Routes.*** This well made map is printed on waterproof and tearproof paper and sells for $7. It covers most of the same routes as the Moab East and West, but at a scale of 1:125,000, it offers even less detail. This map would be good as an overview supplement to go along with some USGS-topos, but is lacking as a stand alone map.

I would say that a better choice from Trails Illustrated is their two ***Canyonlands National Park Maps.*** The two maps, one covering ***Arches and the Island in the Sky District***, and the other, the ***Needles and Maze Districts*** are not mountain bike specific. However, they do cover many of the area's rides and at a scale of 1:50,000, they are about as detailed as you can get shy of the 7.5 minute topos. They do lack coverage of many rides East of Moab such as Porcupine Rim and all of the La Sal Mountains. These maps retail for *$9* each.

Another map that can suffice as an overview is the ***Canyon Country Off Road Vehicle Trail Map for the Moab Area*** by Canyon Country Publications. This map is actually intended for four-wheel '*afficionatos,*' but since most of the area rides are on jeep roads, it is OK for mountain bikers too. I can't tell you what the scale is because they commit a map maker's cardinal sin by leaving out this information. However, it appears to be about 1:100,000. There certainly are better maps available, but for only *$3.50*, this may be the ticket for the biker on a budget.

On my last visit I purchased the ***BLM map for Moab.*** This is a good topographical map that covers a wide area, but is not geared to bikers. I recommend you acquire any of the above maps before getting this one.

Slickrock Trail Maps

There are several maps available that cover the Slickrock Trail. This trail is so well marked and heavily used that a map is actually unnecessary.

However, if you are like me, maps add to the enjoyment of the ride and will also help you to gauge your progress enroute.

First off, I should note there are several free versions of a Slickrock Trail map available at different locations around town including the bike shops and the information center. For the most part, these are adequate. If you want something more functional and also serve as a souvenir, purchase one of the maps described below.

Besides their outstanding Moab East and West, Latitude 40° also distributes a large scale map of the ***Slickrock Trail.*** At a scale of 1:8600 this map has good detail. Unlike their other maps, this one is not topographical, but since the elevation gains and losses on the trail are insignificant, it does not really matter. The Slickrock Trail is superimposed over an aerial photograph of the trail and its surroundings. Although printed on only one side, Latitude 40° has included additional information on the map. One unique feature I like is the locals names and difficulty rating for many of the more technical sections of the trail. The suggested retail for this waterproof and tearproof edition, revised in 1994, is *$7.*

Another map that you might enjoy is the ***Slickrock Bike Trail and Sand Flats Recreation Area*** created by graphic artist Rick Showalter and distributed by Canyon Country Publications. This too is not a topo map. A nice feature of the map is alternate routes that have recently been added to the trail. This map sell for about *$5.00.*

If you are thinking of riding all or part of ***Kokopelli's Trail***, then you should definitely purchase a copy of ***Rick Showalter's*** map of the trail. Although not a true topographical map, Rick's artistic renderings of the relief make it very readable in regards to the terrain. This map is meant to be a compliment to ***Peggy Utesch's Guidebook to the Kokopelli's Trail.*** The price for the map is *$5.00.*

You should be able to find Moab guidebooks in bookstores and bike shops all across the United States, finding maps can be more difficult, however. If you can wait until you get to Moab, you will have several map outlets to choose from.

In Moab, you can find the mountain bike specialty maps literally everywhere, from bike shops, book shops and even at the City Market. The USGS-topo maps are not as readily available, but can be found at either the Information Center or just across the street at **Maps, etc.**

Although many folks don't have a preference, the maps at the Info Center are pre-folded while Maps, etc. keeps them flat.

If are like me and prefer to study maps before arriving on the scene, then two excellent sources of maps are Maps, etc., and Latitude 40°. Both companies publish catalogs featuring numerous maps and guidebooks.

For more information about maps, please contact;

Maps, etc.
29 East Center, Moab, Utah 84532 or call (801) 259-7741

Latitude 40°
P.O. Box 4086, Boulder, Colorado 80306 or call (303) 258-7909.

Where Do I Stay?

Moab visitors have many choices of accomodations, or places to bedding down for the night. If you are interested in camping out you can choose between setting up a basecamp in the backcountry or you can opt for the amenities of a commercial campground. If you preference is for having a roof over your head you will be able to pick from the wide offering of motels, guest houses, B&Bs, condos and even a hostel.

If you've asked me a few years ago, I would have said the obvious choice is to camp out in the backcountry. I still think that if you truly want to immerse yourself in the Moab experience, some camping is in order. There is nothing quite like kicking back in your camp chair and watching the sun go down and the first stars appear over the desert landscape to cap off a perfect day in bikers paradise.

On the down side, so many of us have been camping out in certain areas around Moab that we have had a negative impact on the environment. I still camp out in the Moab backcountry on occasion and recommend that you give it a try. The key is to use minimum impact camping techniques and whenever possible, camp in areas not experiencing overcrowding. You must also keep in mind that new regulations are in effect for certain regions. See the camping section of this chapter for details.

A step up from the free undeveloped campsite is to use one of the developed campgrounds in the National Parks, State Parks, Forest Service or BLM-land. Although these are generally a distance from Moab, most of these campgrounds are located in beautiful locations and are excellent choices to camp with a minimum impact.

Although not my cup of tea due to the lack of privacy and the sterile settings, you can do Moab on the cheap by staying at one of the many commercial campgrounds. Besides minimizing your impact, you will also have a hot shower and other amenities and be centrally located.

When I'm not camping, I tend to gravitate to one of the many motels in town, especially when the weather is foul. I love camping out, but to occasionally have a comfortable bed, a hot shower and maybe a hot tub or swimming pool as a retreat is a real plus. On the down side, I find that I miss many sunsets while relaxing in my room after a good ride and I rarely pull myself out of the bed early enough in the morning to catch the sunrise. As late as a few years ago there was a definite shortage of available rooms in the Moab area. However, with the influx of several large motels, this is no longer the case except during peak periods. You now have the choice of small family run motels with character or large chains with all the amenities.

Up until this year, my Moab stays have been exclusively camping or moteling. While researching this guide, I was amazed at the variety of other accommodations ranging from whole house rentals, B&Bs, condos and even a hostel. I recommend you give these a try. For larger groups, some of these offerings, especially the houses and condos can be the best deals in town while the single traveler or couples can enjoy the intimacy of many of the Bed and Breakfast establishments.

So here they are, motels, campgrounds, and all the rest. I am sure you will find accommodation that will make your stay in Moab a pleasurable experience.

Moab Camping

Until recently, backcountry camping in undeveloped campsites on the public lands surrounding Moab was *derigueur* to fully appreciate the desert experience. There seemed to be an unlimited supply of dispersed campsites along the Sand Flats Road near the Slickrock Trail, along the Kane Creek drainage, on the banks of the Colorado River and elsewhere.

However, as Moab's reputation grew, the number of visitors swelled to the point that all the old campsites were full and impromptu ones were sprouting up like weeds. By the spring of 1994, I was totally blown away while biking to Hurrah Pass along Kane Creek to see scores of camps set up along the creek. This did not quite prepare me for what I saw the next day along the Sand Flats Road where several hundred camps were set up in every nook and cranny along this backcountry thoroughfare.

My first thought was how incredible it was that so many bikers from all over the world were making their pilgrimage to this mountain biker's

Mecca. My next thought was that how long could the fragile desert environment handle this use and abuse? As much as I feel that to truly experience Moab you need to at least camp out in the backcountry for a few days, this was beginning to be too much. We were loving the desert to death.

Fortunately, the Bureau of Land Management, which oversees much of the public lands surrounding Moab, has stepped in and developed a new management plan for the Sand Flats Road and what is referred to as the Colorado Riverway which includes the land along the Colorado River as well as the Kane Creek drainage.

The new regulations require that camping be limited to **designated sites only**. The sites are marked with a brown plastic post with a tent symbol. There are approximately 100 sites along Sand Flats and another 200 along the Riverway. Beginning in the spring of 1995, there will be a charge of *$4* for the use of the Sand Flats sites.

Each site is limited to two vehicles and no more than four tents. Campfires are allowed in existing campfire rings if fire restrictions are not in effect. However, you must bring your own wood supply since wood gathering is prohibited. And, you are not required, but encouraged to use a fire pan to capture your ashes.

The most important new regulation to be aware regarding camping in these areas is you **must now pack out your solid waste**. That means no more shitting in the woods or behind a rock. Get your act together before you leave home and come up with a solid waste disposal system. It can be as basic as a garbage bag lined ammo can with a toilet seat to a self contained port-a-pot. Poison Spider Bikes sells an inexpensive camp toilet for under *$20*.

If you have visited the area before, you might have seen a number of portable out houses about. Do not assume they will be available during your next visit. Currently, they are only in place around Easter vacation and during the Fat Tire Festival. These have been maintained entirely by donations received at the Slickrock Trailhead. Unfortunately, despite an increase in users on the trail, the amount of donations has gone down considerably. It is actually rather pathetic that with approximately 100,000 user days at the Slickrock Trail in 1994, bikers could only fork over about *$2000* in donations.

On the good news side, with the recently enacted day and overnight use fee for the Sand Flats Road, outhouses or perhaps more permanent facilities will become a regular fixture for this popular camping area.

Camping policies are currently posted and enforced. Failure to observe the rules and regulations can result in a fine up to *$1000* and/or up to 12 months in jail. However, the possible fine and jail time should not be the incentive to adhere to these regulations, but rather the desire to minimize your impact on these heavily used areas. I am sure we would all like to have the area be nice the next time we come to visit.

Beyond these two areas with the new restrictions, there are still many areas where regulations are not as strict. Most other lands surrounding Moab that are under the jurisdiction of the Forest Service or BLM allow dispersed camping in undeveloped sites. In the free handout published by BLM titled "*Using Undeveloped Campsites*" the following guidelines for using these primitive sites are requested of all campers.

These sites are all free under the following provisions.

1. That camping at any one site is limited to 14 days per visit.
2. That users pack out their trash.
3. That users avoid camping within 100 feet of springs so that water is accessible to wildlife.
4. That campfires not be left unattended.

The Bureau of Land Management also offers the following minimum impact guidelines.

- Camp at previously used sites if possible. It has been shown that the greatest damage to a campsite occurs during the first few times used. Rather than damage a new area continue to use sites that have already seen use.
- Maintain the beauty of campsites by staying on existing travel routes. Many overused campsites have become centers for ugly networks of trails. Try to stay on the main pathways that lead away from camp.
- Do not put non-burnable items such as cans and bottles into the campfire.
- Do not build new fire rings.
- Use only dead and down wood for campfires. (I say, better yet, do not gather any wood from the desert environment. Either purchase

a bundle of firewood in town or collect a supply from an area in the La Sal National Forest where wood gathering is permitted.

- Burn campfire logs all the way and then douse the coals with water rather than burying.
- Consider using a fire pan so that you can minimize scarring on the ground and then you can pack out the ashes.
- Dispose of human waste properly. Ideally, you should pack out your solid waste although this is not a requirement. In these unrestricted areas the recommended method is to dig a hole six to twelve inches deep, making sure that the site is located well away from streams, campsites and other use areas. You should also pack out your toilet paper in a plastic bag. If you just bury it, animals may dig it up and scatter the paper in the wind.
- Pack out your trash (and a little extra). It goes without saying that you should pack out your own trash, but better yet, take it to the next step and pack out any other trash you find. A good rule of thumb is to leave your campsite in better condition than when you found it.

Another option that is more civilized than using the undeveloped sites, yet more like real camping than using a commercial campground, is utilizing one of the developed sites on BLM or Forest Service land or in one of the National Parks.

These sites all have a use fee and most of them are available on a first come basis. Facilities include picnic tables, restrooms, fire pits and usually running water.

Camping Tips

Many folks journeying to Moab and spending at least part of their time camping are generally experienced campers and have their act together. The following are just a few tips that will help to minimize your impact and make your desert camping experience more enjoyable.

Minimizing your impact.

Most of these tips are found elsewhere in this book but they are so important that they bear repeating.

1. If you would like to have a campfire, you should use a firepan. This allows you to contain and pack our your ashes. An old garbage can lid or metal tray will work just fine.
2. Bring along your own firewood or purchase some in town. In some desert areas gathering wood is strictly prohibited, but even where it is legal, you will still alter the environment. On the other hand, wood gathering where permitted in the La Sal mountains will help to eliminate possible forest fire fuel. I recommend you contact the Forest Service to find out about current restrictions regarding campfires and wood gathering.
3. If you are planning to camp in undeveloped areas, your camping gear should include some type of a port-a-toilet so you can pack out your solid waste. Once again, in some areas this is required, in others it is just good etiquette.

Maximizing your fun.

1. Put a solar shower high on your list of camping accessories. There is nothing like a nice shower after a ride. You could go to town and pay for one, but a solar shower will do just fine. These little wonders work great in any camping environment, but especially so in the desert. In fact, sometimes they work too well. I have returned from warm weather rides only to find my shower too hot. If this should happen, add some cold water to the shower.

If you don't follow my advice on the solar show, take heart, you don't have to be a sleaze ball for the duration of your camp-out. There are several locations in town where shower time can be purchased. Some places are cleaner than others but these standards change from time to time so you will have to check the current situation out yourself. I recommend you asking to see the facilities before plunking down your money. Rates range from $2 to $5 dollars, but cheaper isn't always better as some charge by the minute and others are unlimited.

The locations of shower facilities are as follows:

Canyonlands Campark - 555 South Main
Edge of the Desert - 1251 South Millcreek Dr.
Holiday Haven RV Park - 400 North 500 West

Lazy Lizard Hostel - 1231 South Highway 191
Moab KOA - 3225 South Highway 191
Moab Valley RV & Campark - 1773 North Highway 191
Packcreek Campark - 1520 Murphy Lane
Poison Spider Bicycle Shop - 497 North Main
Portal RV Park and Fishery
Slickrock Campground - 1301 1/2 North Main
Spanish Trail RV and Campark - 2980 South Highway 191
Up the Creek Campground - 210 East 300 South

2. It is a good idea to include several large water containers as part of your camping gear. Very few campsites have water nearby and even if available, might not be potable. By bringing a couple five gallon containers you will minimize the frequency of going to town for refills.

3. A tarp or portable awning can add to your comfort. Since many campsites are short of shade, a little artificial sun protection can go a long way to making your stay more comfortable. It can also give you a refuge in a rainstorm without having to hunker down in your tent.

Campgrounds

I sometimes wondered as I drove by some of Moab's commercial campgrounds who in the hell would stay at places like that. Now, I always knew there was a definite lure for recreational vehicles, but I just couldn't understand why tent campers would forgo the open beauty of the surrounding public lands in exchange for the cramped quarters and lack of privacy that some of these campgrounds offered.

Well, times are changing and while I personally would not stay at most of the commercial campgrounds, they are becoming more of a necessity to help preserve the fragile desert environment. The onslaught of campers to the lands surrounding Moab are loving the desert to death, and while the commercial campgrounds do not offer the "wilderness experience," they are performing a great service by making small plots of Moab available to campers. With the changing BLM regulations limiting and placing certain restrictions on camping along Sand Flats Road and the Colorado Riverway, commercial campgrounds will begin to play a more important role in the region.

In the past few years, several new campgrounds have been added, vastly increasing the total number of available campsites. Although some of the new campgrounds do not look too appealing now, after the shade trees have grown within a few more years, they will begin to look more attractive.

Camping at White Rim campsite.

In addition to alleviating some of the stress on the land, these commercial campgrounds also provide many services and amenities that can make your camp out more pleasurable. Rest rooms, showers and sometimes even swimming pools or hot tubs can make for a more enjoyable experience for the Moab camper.

The following is a brief description of Moab's commercial campgrounds.

Canyonlands Campark

555 South Main - (800) 522-6848 (801) 259-6848

As you first pull up to this campground located in the heart of town it appears to be your typical RV park. From the office you only see rows of RV sites sitting under mature shade trees. However, when you head out to look for the actual tent sites you might be in for a pleasant surprise. Tucked away in the far reaches of the campground are several secluded campsites that might even give you the impression of camping out. Although not all forty tent sites offer this seclusion, they all have shade and a picnic table. Amenities include a swimming pool, showers, BBQs and laundry. Tent sites go for *$14* for two with *$2* for each additional guest. RV sites are *$19*.

Holiday Haven RV Park

400 North 500 West (801)259-5834

The sign at the door said no tent camping and they were also not too friendly.

Kane Springs Campground

P.O. Box 940 (801)259-7821

The Kane Springs Campground is located at the end of the pavement on the Kane Springs Road on the way to Hurrah Pass. I stopped by here several times but never found the manager, who I think just shows up in the evening to collect camping fees. Nevertheless, this is one step above camping at an undeveloped site. For your fee you get outhouses, a table, fire ring and a nice primitive campsite. Some of the sites are shaded but others are totally exposed to the sun. Water is not available. Rates are *$8* for a tent site and there is even a cave for eight that rents for *$25* per night.

Lions Back Campground

No address or phone available

I don't have an address for this primitive campground but it is easy to find. The Lions Back Campground is located on the Sand Flats Road on the way to the Slickrock Trail. It is located right at the base of its namesake, the Lions Back Slickrock. This is another campground where I was unable to roust up a proprietor, but the hand painted signs indicate sites are available for *$8.* Restrooms and water are provided. I haven't seen many people camped here, but with views of the surrounding slickrock, the La Sal mountains and America's most scenic dump it makes for a great location. With the new regulations on the Sand Flats Road business here might begin to pick up. I did notice that voices amplify and echo around the campground, so be careful what you say about your neighbors.

Moab KOA

3225 South Hwy 191 (801) 259-6682

I have never been too big on KOA's, but the Moab version is not too bad as commercial campgrounds go. It does have one of the finer views of the La Sal mountains and the tent sites offer a little more privacy than the average. There are not many mature shade trees, but most picnic tables have an awning for shade. In addition, there is a swimming pool, showers, laundry, gift shop, snack bar, rec room, horseshoe pit and even peewee golf. Tent sites are *$16* for two with *$3* for each additional person with RV sites starting at *$19.*

Moab Valley RV Park

1773 North Highway 191 (801) 259-4469

This is one of the newest campgrounds in Moab as is evidenced by the miniature shade trees. This is also a very friendly place that welcomes mountain bikers. On the south side of the campground are 40 RV sites with full hook-ups, including cable TV; while the north side of camp has 55 tent sites, each with its own patch of green grass. There is a nice view of the surrounding mesas, and in a few more years the shade trees should provide for decent tent sites. In the meantime, plans are underway to build shade coverings for the picnic tables. They currently have one of the cleanest shower facilities I have ever seen. There is also a laundry, BBQs and a volleyball court. Group sites are also available for 20 or more people. Tent sites are $13 for two with $3 for each additional person. RV sites are *$17* for two.

Pack Creek Campground

1520 Murphy Lane (801)259-2982

I thought I was in the ghetto of campgrounds when I first pulled into Pack Creek as the front is pretty run down. However, I did find some nice tree lined tent sites at the far end of the campground along Pack Creek, and their shower facilitates are very clean. Amenities are few, but they do have a laundry and playground. Tent sites are *$13* for two.

Portal RV Park and Fishery

1261 North Hwy 191 (801) 259-7931

This is another of the newer parks which is short on shade until the saplings there begin to mature. It is tucked into a nice area with decent views of the mesas surrounding Moab. To make up for the lack of shade, awnings have been built over the picnic tables at the 10 tent sites. Laundry facilities, snack bar and BBQs are available. A fish pond where one can pay to fish offers a unique feature. Fishing tackle is provided. Tent sites rent for *$10* for up to four people and RV full hook-ups are *$15.50.*

Slickrock Campground

1301 1/2 North Highway 191 (801)259-7660

The Slickrock Campground is another biker friendly place that has 55 tent sites and over 100 RV spaces. Shade is plentiful in this older campground. Some of their many amenities include showers, laundry, BBQs, grocery and gift store, ping pong, horseshoe pits, basketball hoop, swimming pool and three hot tubs. Yes, three hot tubs to soak your tired bones in! Tent sites rent for *$13.50* for two plus *$3* for each extra camper. RV sites run up to $19.25 for full hook-up.

Spanish Trail RV Campground

2980 South Highway 191 (800)787-2751 (801)259-2411

Maybe the manager was having a bad day, but boy, was she rude. I don't know if it was my biker affiliation or what, but the bad vibes were flowing like the Colorado River. Too bad. Maybe, by the time the shade trees have several years to mature the place will become friendlier. If you do stay here, you will be treated to great views of the La Sal mountains from your little piece of grass. Tent sites are *$14.25* for two and RV sites go for *$18.25.*

Up the Creek Campground

210 East 300 South (801)259-2213

Now here is a campground with some character. This small 18 tent site facility located in a residential neighborhood in town is the place with the big t-pee that you see on the way to the Slickrock Trail. For $7 per person you get a nice shaded campsite with a lush green stretch of grass to pitch your tent on. Not a lot of amenities other than picnic tables, clean showers and running water, but I am sure you will enjoy your stay here away from the RVs.

Motels

There has always been quite a few motels in Moab, but until recently, they were for the most part, small family run affairs. With the increase in tourists, brought on in large part by the influx of mountain bikers, a need for more motel rooms became evident. In recent years, several large motels have opened their doors and the total number of beds has increased dramatically.

If you like, you can now pay the bucks and stay in an ultra clean, modern, cookie cutter motel room. For my money, however, I prefer the small operations that have some character. I would rather spend some time shooting the breeze with the owner behind the counter rather than dealing with some uniformed employee working for a large corporation. Of course, this is my personal preference.

There will still be some occasions when you will roll into town and find very few if any rooms available. Make reservations well in advance of your visit, especially during and shortly after Easter vacation, during the Fat Tire Festival or if you arrive in town on a weekend.

I have broken the motel listings into three groups - budget, mid-priced and pricey. Since prices change all the time, I have just listed the motels in these three categories with prices for two adults. **Budget** refers to rooms for under *$50*, **mid-priced** is between *$50 and $75*, and **pricey** is over *$75*. As a standard, I have used the high season prices, which usually occur from sometime in March until November. If you happen to visit Moab in the "off-season", you will find many lodging bargains.

Most motels do not allow bikes in the rooms. Please respect this policy. On the other hand, when bikes are allowed, please have respect for the owners and make every effort not to damage the carpets with chain lube, grease or mud. I appreciate when I can sleep near my bike, so don't spoil this privilege for the next biker that comes along.

Budget Motels

I am a budget traveler by nature, so when I am not camping out near Moab, I will usually stay at one of the mom and pop budget lodgings. Some of these might be considered dives by some, but for my money, they are for the most part good choices. Most mountain bikers should be happy at these inexpensive accommodations. A few amenities are so common that they won't be mentioned unless they are **not** included. These include the availability of non-smoking rooms, cable TV and in-room phones.

The Cottage
488 North Main - (801) 259-5738

The Cottage is not a motel in the traditional sense because it wasn't originally designed as such. Owner John McDonald rents a total of four rooms, three of which look like your typical motel room. The fourth is very unique since it is actually the front half of his home and is furnished as such, complete with family photos on the mantel. Three of the rooms are on the low end of budget with the one room that includes a kitchen falling into the mid-price category. Not much in the way of frills at the Cottage but the rooms are clean and there is a nice shaded grass area where you can set out a picnic. Bikes are not allowed in the rooms, but there is a bike storage area. No phones.

Silver Sage Inn
840 South Main - (801) 259-4420

The Silver sage is another no-frills bargain motel that currently has 17 units with expansion scheduled for 1994. One feature they do have is a decent view of the La Sal mountains from the rooms that face to the east. This is one of the few motels where bikes are still allowed in the rooms and they go one step further by providing rags for bike clean-up.

Hotel Off Cent'R
96 East Center - (800) 237-4685 - (801) 259-4244

As the name implies, this is a hotel rather a motel located near the center of town. All 10 rooms are located upstairs above some local businesses. The bathrooms, a phone and even a community kitchen are located down the hall. Off Cent'R also offers a dorm room with beds going for *$10* per person. Bikes are allowed in the rooms.

Inca Inn Motel
570 North Main - (801) 259-7261

Although I have yet to stay at the Inca Inn, I like this place. The rooms are nothing special, but they are clean and the price is right. An appealing feature is the raised patio next to the swimming pool. This area seems to be popular with the guests for enjoying morning coffee and catching the sunset. Bikes are forbidden in the rooms but a bike lock-up is provided. No in room phones.

Colorado River Lodge
512 North Main - (801) 259-6122

The Colorado River Lodge is one of the older motels in town, but is well maintained. There is a nice grassy area with tables and chairs with a fair view of the surrounding mesas. Bikes are not allowed in the rooms and they do not provide a bike lock-up. If you stay here, you might want to voice your opinion regarding the policy. On the other hand, it is a small one story motel and you can park right in front of your room as a security precaution. They also allow locking bikes to the pillars in front of your room.

Red Rock Lodge
51 North First West - (801) 259-5431/8315

Over the years, I have spent more nights at the Red Rock Lodge than any other establishment. Located off the main highway, this motel is more quiet than most. They have always appeared to cater to the mountain biker crowd as they were one of the first to provide a secured bike storage area. They are also conveniently located right across the street from Moab's original bike shop, Rim Cyclery. Some amenities include an indoor hot tub, in-room refrigerators and HBO. They also have a few rooms where pets are allowed. Many of the rooms have seen a major overhaul in the past few years. The older rooms are still the best buy, while the remodeled ones are a step or two nicer but on the high end of budget.

Prospector Lodge
186 North First West - (801) 259-5145

Other than being in the budget category, there isn't much I can say about this place. Not the cheapest, not the cleanest nor the friendliest, this place doesn't have much going for it. It does have HBO but that isn't saying much. A better name might be the Desperation Inn. If you can't find a room anywhere else, you might try the Prospector. Not especially biker friendly, they do not allow bikes in the rooms or bike storage. While talking to one of the proprietors, I asked if they had any non-smoking rooms. The reply, which came along with a puff of smoke was "we smoke in all the rooms." At least they are located on a quiet street.

Mid-Priced Range

I think that most mountain bikers would be happy at any of the mid-priced motels. Generally, but not always, what you get for the additional money is a slightly larger room that is better furnished than the budget accommodations. Most have either a hot tub or pool and some have both.

Apache Motel
166 South 4th East - (801) 259-5727

Right on the border of budget and mid-priced, the Apache's claim to fame is that John Wayne slept here. You too, can sleep with the spirit of the Duke at this quiet motel located off the main drag. Yes, bikes are allowed in the rooms. Other amenities include a heated swimming pool, HBO and a few kitchen units. A hot tub is also planned for the not too distant future.

Kokopelli Lodge

72 South 100 East - (801) 259-7615

Maybe a bit overpriced considering there is neither a swimming pool nor hot tub, but the Kokopelli is a definite biker friendly lodge. Of course, this means bikes are allowed in the rooms, but this label is also because of Mel and Barb, the motel's friendly managers. One Kokopelli feature is that it is located on a quiet side street. This means no semi-trucks roaring down the road at 3:00 am. The rooms have recently been remodeled and are very light and cheery. There is also a popular picnic area complete with BBQ for guest use.

Virginian Motel

70 East 200 South - (800) 261-2063 (801) 259-5951

It wasn't that long ago that the Virginian was a budget motel, but times have changed and so have the prices. At least they are on the low end of this category. The Virginian, which is located about a half block off the main drag features 20 older units with kitchenettes and 17 new rooms. All the rooms have recently been redecorated. Bikes are allowed in the rooms. Other guest amenities include free HBO and a BBQ and picnic table.

The Red Stone Inn

535 South Main - (800) 772-1972 (801) 259-3500

This is a new motel that has some personality and also looks like it should be more expensive than it is. There is no pool or spa, but I was told that a hot tub is in the works. Manager Sandy Bastian let me know that they love to cater to the biking industry, which was partially evident by allowing bikes in the rooms and also providing rags for clean-up. All rooms have a kitchenette equipped with a refrigerator, microwave, coffee pot and small sink. In addition there is also a guest laundry and a gas BBQ and picnic area.

Rustic Inn

120 East First South - (800) 231-8184 (801) 259-6177

The Rustic Inn is another of the side street motels. Some of the 35 units are only a few years old, with the rest redecorated and refurnished. Bikes are not allowed in the rooms but a storage area is provided. Amenities include HBO, heated swimming pool, guest laundry room and a continental breakfast if you like to start your day with donuts and coffee. On the down side, local phone calls cost 25¢.

JR's Inn
1075 So Highway 191 - (801) 259-8352/6979

If you are looking for a motel with many amenities this is not the place. If, on the other hand, your priorities lean toward a nice room, then JR's might be for you. Considering what you get, this little 10 unit motel seems pricey to me, but six of the rooms come with semi-kitchenettes and all are large, clean and well furnished in a southwest style. They do provide bike storage.

Bowen Motel
169 North Main - (800) 874-5439 (801) 259-7132

The Bowen is one of those motels that has recognized mountain bikers as a solid core of its customers. They are unique in that they have a bike storage area, but if you really want to sleep near your bike, you can fork over an additional buck a bike to wheel your baby into your room. Nice concept. The rooms are large and clean and the cable TV includes HBO and ESPN. The Bowen also has a heated swimming pool.

Days Inn
426 N. Main St - (800) 329-7466 (801) 259-4468

Sure it is a chain, but the folks at the front desk seem to be friendly. The rooms are as you might expect - large and clean. You get many extras for your dollars including a heated pool, indoor hot tub, HBO, Showtime and a daily continental breakfast. You are not allowed to bring your bike into your room, but you can lock it up in a storage area.

Moab Travelodge
550 South Main - (800) 325-6171 (801) 259-6171

Are they bike friendly or not? If you read their brochure you see that they welcome bicyclists to slickrock bike country and they say they can meet all our special needs. On the other hand, bikes are not allowed in the rooms and no lock-up is available. I think they need to work this contradiction out. It is a nice place, as you would expect for the money and the second floor rooms have decent La Sal views. However, the view would be no consolation if someone was to rip off your bike while you slept! They do have an outdoor heated swimming pool and the cable TV includes HBO.

Pricey

Personally, I do not like to spend too much on a motel room. I usually travel on a lean budget and my theory is that I am going to be out and about most if not all of the day and I would rather take the money I save on a room for better meals. Besides, once you turn off the lights, it is hard to tell the cheap room from the expensive unless there are bugs in your bed. I do, however, know many well to do mountain bikers that can afford to and do stay at the high end establishments.

During my research I found that a goodly number of the high end motels in Moab had very little concern for mountain bikers and their bikes. None of them allowed bikes in the rooms which came as no surprise. What disappointed me was the lack of lockable bike storage at many of these establishments. These are also the same large motels where bike thieves have the best chance of ripping off bikes without being detected. If you must stay at these places, express your disappointment at their lack of storage facilities.

Sunset Motel
41 West 100 North - (800) 421-5614 (801) 259-5196

Is this a typo or what? What is the Sunset Motel doing in the pricey category? For $75 or more a night, this is a dive. I guess you could say it is rustic and unique, but upon inspecting the rooms you would think it would be in the budget category. Maybe with some landscaping and new room furnishings it might belong in the mid-price category, but not the high end. I don't know why bikes are not allowed in these rooms, and they provide a less than secure bike storage in the laundry room. They do have a swimming pool and HBO.

Super 8 Motel
889 N. Main - (801) 259-8868

With 146 units, the Super 8 is the largest motel in Moab. I cannot say much more about this cookie cutter motel than this. No, they do not allow bikes in the rooms. As somewhat of a concession to mountain bikers they do provide a bike rack to lock your steed to, but it is outside exposed to the elements. Amenities include hot tub, heated swimming pool, guest laundry, and HBO. It is clean and modern but totally lacks character. Not my kind of place, especially at these prices. By the way, if you drive up to the office, do not pull up under the entry way if you have bikes on the roof. There is very low clearance at the entrance and from the scars on the overhang, it appears that more than a few bikes have smashed into this low lying bike trap.

Moab Valley Inn

711 South Main - (800) 831-6622 (801) 259-4419

It is big, modern and beautiful but not very bike friendly. No bikes in the rooms and no bike lock-up! The rooms are large and well furnished and the pool and spa are wonderful but they do not seem to be biker friendly. This is another of those big parking lot affairs where your bikes are targets for rip-offs. What can I say? If and when they get a bike lock-up this will be a great choice with bikers with bucks or on an expense account.

Landmark Motel

168 North Main Street - (800) 441-6147 (801) 259-6147

It's not so big, not so modern but still a very nice motel, yet once again not very biker friendly. Bikes are not allowed in the rooms and a bike lock-up is not provided. Is this beginning to sound familiar? What they do have is a heated pool, hot tub, HBO, and guest laundry to go along with their large, clean rooms. There are not, however, any non-smoking rooms.

Comfort Suites, Moab

800 South Main St. - (800) 228-5150 (801) 259-5252

If you are going to pay the big bucks, then the Comfort Suites would be an excellent choice. This is definitely one of the best digs in town and they **do** have a bike lock-up! The rooms are some of the best in town in regards to size, furnishings and extras including microwaves and refrigerators. Other amenities include an indoor swimming pool, hot tub, fitness room, guest laundry, continental breakfast and HBO. Other features include a fax service, copy machine and conference room. In addition, the rooms that face the highway should have a decent view of the La Sal mountains.

Best Western Greenwell Motel

105 South Main St. (801) 259-6151

Just like any Best Western motel, the standards of the rooms are above average. This Best Western currently has an outdoor pool with plans for the addition of a hot tub, fitness room and covered bike storage. Currently, they only have bike racks to lock up your bike. Some of the rooms come with a refrigerator and all have HBO.

Best Western Canyonlands Inn
16 South Main (801) 259-2300

The other Best Western in town is another pricey facility that is pro-bike. Not only do they have a bike lock-up, but they even have an area where you can work on your bike. They have a very nice hot tub and swimming pool that is covered in the colder months. Other amenities include a fitness room, game room, guest laundry, continental breakfast, HBO, ESPN, fax service, copy machine, and conference room.

Ramada Inn
182 South Main (800) 2-RAMADA (801) 259-7141

The Ramada is one of those places where you can drop a hundred dollar bill for the night and to be honest with you, I am not so sure what the attraction is unless you are on an expense account. On the plus side, they do provide a bike lock-up. They also have a heated pool, hot tub, HBO and a large conference room.

Bed & Breakfast + Guest Houses

Tucked away along the back streets of Moab are several Bed and Breakfast and guest house establishments. I have lumped these two categories together as some of the establishments that call themselves B&Bs are actually what I consider guest houses and some of the guest houses appear to be B&Bs.

The common denominator here is that you are renting rooms in an occupied house. Sometimes breakfast is included and sometimes it is not. The Moab B&Bs cover a wide spectrum, from what you would traditionally expect in a B&B to the rental of someone's spare rooms along with a breakfast.

The rates quoted here are for peak season with two people in a room. Since many rooms in a particular home vary, in size and bathroom availability, the rates also vary depending on the room. Just like the motels, many of these establishments offer an off-season discount. A few however, maintain the same price on a year round basis and some shut down during the winter.

Just like everything else in this "discovered" town, the Bed and Breakfast and guest house establishments are undergoing change. While doing research for this book, several of the B&Bs were for sale. With new ownership, there may be changes in prices and amenities. Stay tuned.

Canyon Country Bed & Breakfast
590 North 500 West - (800) 435-0284 (801) 259-5262

Canyon Country is Moab's oldest B&B and perhaps the most popular with mountain bikers. This sprawling ranch style home is located in a quiet residential neighborhood. The active lifestyle theme is carried on in the decor with a fine collection of original photographs as well as an adventure travel library. The house features five rental rooms, three with full bath, one with a half bath and the other with a shared bath. Breakfasts are hearty, wholesome and nutritious. Amenities include an outdoor hot tub and a VCR. A whole house rental is available for groups up to 14. Rates range from *$55 to $70* per night.

Sunflower Hill Bed and Breakfast
185 North 300 East - (801) 259-2974

If you are looking for an ultra "cutesy" B&B, the Sunflower Hill is probably right up your alley. Maybe a little too cutesy for my tastes, this nearly 100 year old renovated farmhouse is definitely a B&B in the traditional sense. Each room is uniquely decorated and features a queen bed, private bath, color television and air conditioning. When it comes to breakfast, owners Richard and Marjorie Stucki, serve what I have been told is the best in town. The Sunflower also has a lush garden, outdoor hot tub, adventure library and secure bike storage. Rates range from *$64 to $86* in season.

Mayor's House Bed and Breakfast
505 Rose Tree Lane - (801) 259-3019

The Mayor's House is just as the name implies, the home of Moab's Mayor. This fine B&B is one of Moab's most spacious and luxurious modern homes. The rooms include four with shared bath, a master bedroom which includes a jacuzzi tub and a family suite that features a kitchen, game room, large screen TV and a shower for two. Amenities outside in the beautifully landscaped yard include a hot tub, swimming pool with lap lane, and patio with BBQ. Locked bike storage is provided. Rates range from *$65* for shared bath to *$125* for the suite.

Spanish Trail Inn B&B
3180 Spanish Trail Rd. (801) 259-4377

Located south of town near the golf course, the Spanish Trail Inn offers peace and quiet in a secluded setting. Most rooms have a shared bath but the master suite features a king bed, private balcony and jacuzzi. Although the two acre grounds could use some landscaping, it does include an aviary and fish pond. I did not note a lockable bike storage area, but its private setting probably means that your bikes should be OK on your car. This is also the only B&B that allows smoking in some rooms. The upstairs rooms are smoke free, however. Rates are from *$45 to $95*.

Circle A Ranch Bed and Breakfast
128 West 200 North St. (801) 259-7632

They call themselves a B&B but in reality, they are more like a condo with optional organic breakfast provided at an additional charge of $5 per person. The Circle A features two small condo units that can accommodate up to six. The place doesn't look like much from the outside, but the rooms are very clean and well maintained. The yard could use some work, but it does have a hot tub and comfortable chairs and hammock to kick back in. One unique feature is that the units each have a fireplace. I assume that firewood is provided. Bike storage is available. The price is *$60* for two with discounts for stays of three or more nights.

Pioneer Springs Bed and Breakfast
1275 South Boulder Ave (801) 259-4663

The Pioneer Springs is one of Moab's newer B&Bs. Located on the south end of town and west of the highway, the Pioneer is tucked at the base of the red rock walls bordering town. The grounds are outstanding and feature a swimming pool and plenty of green grass and shade trees. Breakfast is served each morning on the patio that has a great view of the Moab Valley. You can also enjoy this same view from the hot tub. The rooms are nothing special, and since they are in the basement, they tend to be dark and cool. The community room has cable TV, VCR and a pool table. A dirt road behind the yard can lead you to the Kane Creek Boulevard and access to the mountain bike routes off this road. Bikes are allowed in the rooms. Rates range from *$50 to $60* and rental of the entire basement is possible.

The Desert Chalet Bed and Breakfast
1275 E. San Juan Drive (801) 259-5793

Although not located in the best of neighborhoods, the Desert Chalet has become a haven for visiting mountain bikers. This unique log home features a variety of rooms, most with shared bath. Owner Marcia Medford is well traveled and loves to host visitors from all over the world. Amenities include hot tub, outside deck with BBQ, and the use of kitchen and laundry facilities, VCR and stereo. Bike storage is available in the garage. Rates range from *$50 to $75* for two and you can also rent the entire house.

Purple Sage Bed and Breakfast

1150 Sage St. - (801) 259-3310

The Purple Sage is located just around the corner from the Desert Chalet, meaning the neighborhood is not the best, but this newly constructed log cabin makes for a comfortable getaway. Four of the five rooms are relatively spacious, but watch your head if you rent the low ceilinged loft. Bike storage is available and rates range from *$55 to $80.* You can also rent the entire house for *$250* for up to 14 people.

Red Valle Bed and Breakfast

210 East 100 North - (801) 259-5408

Tom and Lilly Ann Balsley, who also rent 10 mobile homes, have opened up two rooms in their house for rent as a B&B. I actually consider this more of a guest room situation than B&B, but a continental breakfast if provided. The rooms are large and clean, but nothing to write home about. Bike storage is available. Rates are *$50* per night.

Kane Creek Bed and Breakfast

490 Kane Creek Blvd. - (801) 259-7345

This is another guest room situation going by the title of B&B. What the Kane Creek lodging has going for it is a good location and wonderful views of the La Sals from the patio. The only notable feature of the 2 bedrooms is that one has hideous red carpet and the other not quite so hideous yellow carpet. The red room also has a TV. The price is *$55* for yellow and *$65* for red.

Sandi's Bed and Breakfast

450 Walker St. - (801) 259-6359

I'm not sure what is up here. When I introduced myself over the phone as a writer working on a mountain bikers guide to Moab, they decided they didn't want to show me the place. Are they anti-biker? You be the judge of that.

Matterhorn Guest House
3601 E. Matterhorn Heights - (801) 259-8352

This wasn't the easiest place to find, but it was worth the search. You will not find any E. Matterhorn Heights on a map or road sign and there is no sign for the Matterhorn Guest House, but just hone in on the large white house above Spanish Valley with the seven portals and you will be able to make your way to this spectacular home with rooms for rent. My suggestions is that you stay here soon as the owners are thinking of getting out of the business. This large house commands one of the best views in Moab and has been landscaped to perfection. Two of the three rooms rent for *$75* but lack a view. The one with the great vista goes for *$85*. Of course, everyone has access to the patios to soak in the sights.

DeLong Guest House
368 Walker - (801) 259-7651

Host Lulu DeLong says that she rarely gets any bikers staying at her spilt level home on a quiet residential street. Staying here might be more like visiting your parents or grandparents. The two rental rooms share the bath and rent for *$60* each.

Millcreek Inn
497 Millcreek Drive - (801) 259-8524/7014

When the rental room shortage became pronounced in Moab, Ruby and Val Thompson opened up their home to the many visitors to Moab. Four years later they still enjoy hosting tourists in their "home away from home" atmosphere. They only rent two basic rooms, but each morning you will be treated to a full breakfast. At only *$40* per night, this is quite a deal. Bike storage is provided. The Millcreek Inn is the closet rental facility to the Slickrock Trail.

Moab Guest House
300 West 400 North - (801) 259-4457

The Moab guest house is only available on a nightly basis during the summer months. The rest of the year it is a monthly rental and not available to mountain bikers during their prime spring and fall seasons.

Condos, Houses, etc.

Beyond the motel and B&B scene, there lies a small reservoir of other miscellaneous rentals that the Moab traveler can seek in accommodations. These range from condos, houses, mobile homes and even an international hostel.

Most of these come with full or almost full kitchens, so if you plan on staying for some time, this gives you the opportunity to prepare some home cooking while on the road. For groups of four or more, they also tend to be a good bargain.

Condos

So what is a condo, anyway? I always had this impression of fancy vacation apartments that were designed, built and furnished with the vacation traveler in mind. This was not necessarily the case in Moab. Most of the condos I inspected started their life as apartments complexes and have been converted to overnight and weekly rental as the needs (and money making potential) dictated. It is great that these facilities are now available to the Moab traveler, but on the other hand, by taking these apartments off the local rental market, this has added to the low cost housing shortage in the area.

If you can live with that, then you will find some great deals and accommodations to be had in this category.

Fandago Guest House
140 South 200 East (PO Box 1295) - (801) 259-8921

The Fandago is a four-plex located just two blocks from the center of town on a lovely quiet side street. Each unit has two bedrooms and comes with VCR, air-conditioning, and complete kitchen facilities which includes a microwave. Outside they have a guest BBQ and lockable bike storage. Although pets are not allowed in the condos, they do provide a fenced dog run in the back yard. This is a real comfortable place and I am sure you will enjoy kicking back on the front porch under the shade of the many trees. Rates are *$60* for two and *$5* for each additional guest. In addition, if you stay a week, the seventh night is free. For larger groups they can provide extra futons.

Nichols Lane Accommodations
543 Nichols Lane - (801) 259-5047

Another peaceful setting is the Nichols Lane Accommodations and an outstanding bargain to boot. This is another four-plex with one and two bedroom units which can accommodate up to five guests. Although the furnishings are on the older side, it doesn't detract from the setting. The units are well maintained, commodious and include full kitchens. Outside there is a hot tub and a comfortable patio area with BBQ. A bike locker is provided. Rates range from *$45* for two people to *$50* for five.

Cedar Breaks Condos
Center and 400 East - (801) 259-7830

All six of the Cedar Breaks units have two bedrooms and can sleep up to six guests. The furnishings are great and the walls have been decorated with many outstanding photos taken by the owner. In a slight twist off the B&B theme, breakfast ingredients are provided and can be prepared in the fully equipped kitchen. The complex also includes laundry facilities. Bikes are allowed in the rooms. Rates are *$70* for two and *$10* for each additional guest.

Cottonwood Condos
338 East 100 South - (800) 447-4106 (801) 259-8897

The Cottonwood has eight spacious one bedroom units. Although they are roomy, there is a limit of four people. All the condos are light and airy, with the upstairs rentals especially so. Each condo has a queen bed in the bedroom and a sofa sleeper in the living room. Besides a full kitchen with microwave there is also a cable TV with VCR and access to the owners huge video library. (He used to own a video rental store.) Bikes are allowed in the rooms. Rates are *$55* for two and *$5* for each additional guest.

Westwood Guest House
81 East 100 South - (800) 526-5690 (801) 259-7283

Although the Westwood has its charm, it was not my favorite. However, the folks that stay there keep coming back so that says something. All units have one bedroom and can accommodate up to nine guests. In my opinion, the upstairs units were superior with more light, privacy and balconies. The fully equipped kitchens include the food necessary to prepare a hearty breakfast. Out back there is a patio area that includes a hot tub. Rates are *$59* for two and *$10* for each extra person. If you stay for a week, the seventh night is free.

The Rose Tree Inn

481 Rose Tree Lane (800) 421-5614 (801) 259-5196

The Rose Tree claims that it is simply Moab's finest apartment/condo type lodging. If you just judged by price, I would have to agree. Don't get me wrong, this is a very nice place with fine furnishings and a comfortable feel, but it is pricey. (Once again, my budget traveler roots are showing.) Nevertheless, if you can afford it, I am sure you will enjoy your stay. Amenities include complete kitchen, daily maid service, cable TV with remotes and HBO, AC, laundry room, locked bike storage, southwest decor, outdoor hot tub, BBQ and a quiet residential setting. Their brochure states there is a large heated pool, which I couldn't find. I was later told that you could use the pool at the Sunset Motel located some distance away. Bogus! Rates start at *$89* for two.

The Ron Tez

450 East 200 South (801) 259-7599/7273

The Ron Tez is at or near the bottom of my list of Moab's unique accommodations. The two bedroom apartments are roomy, but are decorated in early Salvation Army. Don't ask me why bikes are not allowed in the rooms as just about any old dirty mountain bike would spruce up the decor. To make matters worse, a bike lock-up is not provided. The amenity is a small BBQ that can be shared between the 8 units. They do not even include phones. Price is *$60* per night. With some work and investment this could be a good place to stay, but for now, I would keep looking.

Red Valle Homes

201 East 100 North (801) 259-5408

The Red Valle rents 10 mobile homes located off a centrally located yet peaceful residential street. When I first realized that I was checking out mobile homes, I must say that my expectations were low. Was I in for a surprise. For groups of four to eight, these are some of the best deals in town. Several of the mobile homes are brand new and even the older ones have been well maintained. The furnishings, especially in the newer units are first rate. All the units come with full kitchens, AC, washer and dryer, and cable TV with several premium channels. They all have a small covered patio and grassy area outside. Bike lockers are available and in a central area there is a hot tub, above ground pool and patio picnic area. I was told that several movie stars have stayed here, during location shoots in the Moab area. The dayly summer rates for a 14"x80" trailer range from *$80* to about *$110.*

Sundance Condo

208 East 200 South - (801) 259-8429

The Sundance is only a summer rental and I did not have an opportunity to see what they have to offer.

Slickrock House

1121 Jackson Street - (801) 259-4275

The Slickrock House is a comfortable four bedroom, two bath house rental that can accommodate up to eight. This fully furnished home includes TV, stereo, laundry facilities, wood stove, AC, and BBQ. The front porch runs the length of the house and is a great spot to kick back and relax after a ride. The rate is *$125* for up to four with an additional *$10* for each additional person. There is also a two night minimum and weekly discount.

Slickrock Inn

286 South 400 East (801) 259-2266

The Slickrock Inn is another whole house rental located in the heart of Moab. This old house used to be a bed and breakfast and has character evidenced by the sloping floors and creaking floorboards. I'm not sure why the owners got out of the B&B business as this seems to be the perfect type of house for this kind of operation. It does seem to be a comfortable house to rent, but is a bit pricey. A good news, bad news feature is that there is no TV. There is a full kitchen, and a comfortable backyard with BBQ and volleyball court. Don't hit the ball too hard, however, or you will spend the day hopping fences after balls. There is not a secured bike area, but there is a covered bike rack in the backyard. The cost is *$125* for four for just the downstairs and *$225* for the entire house which can handle up to 10.

Big Tree Cottage

310 East 100 South (801) 259-5764

If you would like to rent a house and still have money for meals, then the Big Tree Cottage is the deal for you. This quiet little cottage is located next to the biggest cottonwood in town just a couple blocks from downtown. This one bedroom house can accommodate up to four with a queen-sized bed in the bedroom and a sofa sleeper in the living room. The kitchen is well equipped and the TV also has a VCR. You will enjoy kicking back on the patio which has a BBQ. During season, you can also help yourself to vegetables and herbs from the garden. Rates are *$45* for two and *$50* for four. Weekly rates are also available.

Cedar Hills Guest House

3431 Juniper Dr. (801) 259-5135

Although beyond my usual budget, this house in Cedar Hills above Spanish Valley was one of the finest places that I visited. This simple three bedroom home has been completely remodeled and decorated with a modern kitchen and southwest furnishings. I loved the house, but I enjoyed the view of the La Sal mountains and the surrounding slickrock even more. If you can afford it, and you don't mind being away from the hustle of town, then this is the place. Amenities include phones, laundry, cable TV and a BBQ. On the down side, there is no bike lock-up, yet. I did suggest this to the owners and they will be adding a storage shed at some point in time. In the meantime, please don't bring your dirty bikes in the house. The carpets are so new and the house is so clean it would be a crime. In addition, the house is on such a quiet street that your bikes should be OK locked up outside to the bike rack. The price for this great rental is *$105* for two, *$120* for four and *$150* for six.

Shiloh Country Inn

2390 Old City Park Rd. (801) 259-8684

This unique lodging is located off the beaten path in Spanish Valley south of town. Currently, there is an outbuilding with five rentals, some with private bath and some with shared bathrooms. There is also a main building with rooms that are sometimes rented. The rooms are nothing special and are relatively cheap, but not cheap enough. There is some potential for this place and since the Inn was for sale during my visit, maybe new owners will take this place to the next level. Rooms range from *$45* to *$65* for two.

Lazy Lizard International Hostel

1213 South Highway 191 (801) 259-6057

Tucked away in an industrial district south of town is the Lazy Lizard International (not just for youth) Hostel. If you can't afford a motel or condo and you don't want to camp out this could be the place for you. The facilities include community kitchen, TV with VCR and movie library, laundry, showers and hot tub. Dorm rooms rent for *$7*, private rooms *$20* for two, private cabins *$30* for four and campsites for *$4* per person.

The City Market.

Wine and Dine in Moab

Even before being discovered by mountain bikers, Moab had all the trappings of a tourist town, catering to visitors to the National Parks and the Colorado River. Just like any tourist town, Moab had a decent variety of restaurants to choose from. However, since the biker boom of the past ten years, many new eateries have opened up, giving visitors an even wider range of choices.

As is the case with most tourist towns, the restaurant business is usually in a state of flux. While many restaurants have become local institutions, others are here today and gone tomorrow; and what you might enjoy on one visit might be a disaster the next. I experienced this not too long ago.

On a fall trip our group was on a quest for the best burger in Moab. Thanks to a tip from a couple employees at the Kaibab Bike Shop, we found it. Of the nine people in our party, we ordered eight different kinds of burgers and they all received two thumbs up. Less than six months later, I returned with a few other carnivore friends only to find that the restaurant was under new ownership. The menu had changed dramatically and our burger selection was limited. I could have lived with that, but the quality had also gone out the door and we walked away after our meal unsure of where the best burger in Moab was located. Talk about a whine and dine experience.

Fortunately, with the opening of the ***Slickrock Cafe***, I can bestow this crown on the new king in town, the Uranium Burger.

Whether on a tight budget or an expense account, you are sure to find something to fit your needs and fill your stomach. From greasy spoons to healthy new age yuppie vegetarian, the choice is yours.

I have not even come close to sampling all the restaurants in town. Many that I have tried over the years have not remained consistent. Other than a casual comment or two, I have not attempted to review or criticize the food quality, service or ambiance. What I have done is listed most of the restaurants along the type of food they serve. The rest is up to you. I recommend that you pick up a copy of the *Moab Menu Guide* that is available free all over town. The Menu Guide doesn't review the restaurants, but it does list the menus for over half the eateries in town.

In future editions of this book I would like to review restaurants with a more critical eye. If you have any comments, pro and con, on any restaurants that you try during your visit, we would appreciate hearing from you.

Arches Pancake Haus
182 South Main - (801) 259-7141

Open from 6 AM to 10 PM daily, the Pancake Haus serves your typical family fare of hearty breakfasts to meat and potatoes dinners.

Beaudean's Dream Cafe
690 South Main - (801) 259-2253

This bakery and coffee shop opens at 6 AM and is a great place for caffeine consumption.

The Branding Iron
2971 South Highway 191 - (801) 259-6275

This cowboy bar and restaurant primarily serves lunches and dinners. They also have a few breakfast items on the menu, but with an 11 AM opening they cater to the late rising crowd. The menu mostly features cooked sandwiches. Before becoming the Branding Iron, it used to be the home of the best burgers in town. It has gone down a few notches in my book.

Cafe Ruisseau
125 South Main - (801) 259-2599

The Cafe Ruisseau serves what they refer to as traditional cuisine. This includes steaks, seafood, pasta and a few specialties. Breakfast and lunch are also served beginning at 6 AM.

Catarina's (dinner only)
51 North Main - (801) 259-6070

If you are looking to carbo load, Catarina's selection of Italian dishes and pizza might be a good choice. Catarina's opens at 5:00 PM for dinner only.

Cattleman's Restaurant and Lounge
1991 South Highway 191 - (801) 259-6585

Cattleman's is located at the Dar-C Truck Plaza which brings two old wives tales to mind. One is if the truckers eat there the food must be good. The other is never eat at a truck stop. You can use whichever theory you want to go with. If you opt for the former, you will find the restaurant is open 24 hours and serving typical diner fare.

Center Cafe (dinner only)
92 East Center Street - (801) 259-4295

If your wallet is bigger than your appetite, then you will enjoy the California style cuisine served at the Center Cafe. Dinners only.

Center Court
686 South Main - (801) 259-2524

Here is your chance to watch a game while dining, although don't get your hopes up that the prime sporting event of the day will necessarily be on because it might be preempted by an infomercial. All you do-it-yourselfers will enjoy the cook-your-own entrees. At least you won't have to wash the dishes.

City Market
425 South Main - (801) 259-5181

No listing of Moab restaurants would be complete without mentioning City Market.Whether you are looking for breakfast, lunch, dinner or a midnight snack, you will be able to find something to please your palette at the C.M. The City Market is open 24 hours and features a bakery, deli, and perhaps the best salad bar in town. No reservations required.

Creekside Restaurant
105 South Main - (801) 259-6151

Mexican-American foods are featured at the Creekside Restaurant.

Dos Amigos Mexican Cantina/Rumors Cafe and Bakery
56 East 300 South - (801) 259-7903

Two restaurants in one, what a concept. For some unknown reason, the Rumors Cafe (or what used to be known as the Big Ear) is now under the same roof with Dos Amigos. I haven't been in since the merger, but I guess you can now get a burrito and a burger at the same time. I had eaten at Dos Amigos a few times and found the Mexican food adequate but nothing to write home about.

Fat City Smoke House
36 South 100 West - (801) 259-4302

Meat eaters will love the Texas style barbecue offered at Fat City. Although their "not so famous" sauce is on the tame side, the ribs are cooked to perfection. There is even a vegetarian section on the menu for the tofu crowd.

Golden Stake
540 South Main - (801) 259-7000

The Golden Stake claims to be the *"home of real food"* and *"where the locals choose to eat."* I'm not sure what *"real food"* is or if I have ever eaten it. The Golden Stake features steak and potato dinner fare as well as basic dinner breakfasts and lunches.

Gonzo Cafe
606 South Main Street

The Gonzo Cafe offers your new age diner fare, including burritos, falafels, and burgers (vege and real). This is also one of the best places in town to start your day with one of their omelets or grilled bagel sandwiches. I have also been told by caffeine addicted friends that this is one of the best places in town to fuel up with a gourmet blend. A unique offering of the Gonzo Cafe is their Spoon and Tune. While you eat, you can have your bike safety checked at the World University of Cycling, which is in the same building.

Grand Old Ranch House
1266 North Highway 191 - (801) 259-5753

One of Moab's finer dining experiences can be had at the historic Grand Old Ranch House. Beyond their surf and turf offerings you will find a unique selection of German entrees.

Honest Ozzie's and Desert Oasis
60 North 100 West - (801) 259-8442

I have yet to talk to anyone that was not satisfied with a meal at Honest Ozzie's. Serving breakfast, lunch, and dinner, Honest Ozzie's is sort of your hippie style vegetarian restaurant that serves some meat items. Their Burrito Mondo can compete for the best burrito in town.

Jailhouse Cafe
101 North Main - (801) 259-3900

The Jailhouse is another of the newer additions to the Moab restaurant scene and they seem to be off to a great star. The folks at the Jailhouse are some of the friendliest in town.Breakfasts are their specialty (good, but not what you would call hearty portions).

JB's Restaurant and Bakery
811 South Main - (801) 259-2646

For you "all you can eat" types, JB's might be the place. Besides the usual breakfast, lunch and dinner offerings, they have a breakfast buffet and on weekends all you can eat prime rib dinner.

JR's
1075 South Highway 191 - (801) 259-8352

JR's claims to be the finest restaurant and inn, but that might be a stretch. This is a roadside diner, nothing more, nothing less.

Kayenta Coffee House
92 East Center - (801) 259-2553

The Kayenta Coffee House is primarily a caffeine distributor. They also have a bakery and deli, but most of those items are pricey. Considering they are a coffee house you would think that they would have the bean scene down.

La Cocina Catering
Cart Location - Corner of 100 West and Walnut Lane

Susan McDaniel, who has been catering special events and parties in Moab, has set up a roach coach on a quiet corner along 100 West. Susan's menu is limited but her black bean burritos and vege burgers are top notch.

La Hacienda
574 North Main - (801) 259-6319

I thought that I had visited every Mexican restaurant in town. How did I miss this place on Main street. My mouth is watering while reading the menu that ranges from basic fare to Mexican specialties. They do offer a selection "for the gringo" which worries me some. Check it out and you decide.

Eddie McStiff's
57 South Main - (801) 259-BEER

You will always find a hoard of mountain bikers hanging out at this eatery and brew pub. Several of my friends call this their favorite Moab restaurant. I am not sure if this is due to the wide offering of foods or the fine selection of brew. The menu includes pasta, pizza, southwestern cuisine and even stir fry. Although not one of their featured selections, their burgers are in the upper echelon.

Parking lot of Eddie McStiff's Brew Pub. A biker hangout.

Milt's Stop and Eat
356 Millcreek Drive - (801) 259-7424

Milt's offers a good place to grease up on your way to the Slickrock Trail. This little diner serves your typical greasy spoon fare. I enjoyed their slow cooked breakfast, but had to rush through my meal to get out of the second hand cigarette smoke that hangs in the air.

Mi Vida Restaurant
900 North Highway 191 - (801) 259-7146

The Mi Vida's claim to be "above the rest" is warranted as it sits perched overlooking town in the former home of Moab's millionaire/prospector Charles Steen. Another one of Moab's finer dining experiences; and if the food doesn't meet your expectations, at least the view is guaranteed to please.

Moab Diner
189 South Main - (801) 259-4006

The Moab Diner is a restaurant and ice cream shop. They feature "real home cooking." I'm not sure if this means that they cook at home and bring the food into the restaurant or if the owners live in the restaurant. A big plus for mountain bikers, or anyone that breathes for that matter, is that no smoking is allowed.

Pasta Jays
4 South Main - (801) 259-2900

Located smack in the center of town, Pasta Jays offers up a good carbo load at a decent price. While the sauces are not up to my grandmother's or mother's standards, they are tasty. Dining on the outdoor patio on a warm evening is a treat as long as you don't mind the occasional waif of exhaust fumes.

Poplar Place - Pub and Eatery
100 North Main Street - (801) 259-6018

Mexican food, pasta, pizza, and beer - what more could a biker ask for. I have always enjoyed my meals at the historic Poplar Place. Just don't sit under the swamp cooler upstairs or you might get hypothermia.

The Rio Colorado
100 West 2nd South - (801) 259-6666

For one reason or another, I have dined at the Rio on most of my visits.The Mexican food is good and it comes in quantity. Take my advice— when eating at a Mexican restaurant, stick with the Mexican food. I tried their burger and was unimpressed.

Slickrock Cafe
Center and Main - (801) 259-8004

The Slickrock Cafe, one of the newest restaurants in town, is one of those new age, yuppified, casual diners. But what can I say, I loved it. The walls are adorned with replicas of petroglyphs and photos from some local photographers. This in itself is almost worth the visit; but the garlic and blue cheese laden uranium burger will bring me back.

Sundowner Restaurant
1393 North Highway 191 - (801) 259-5201

The Sundowner serves dinner only, opening each evening at 5 PM. Their menu covers a wide array of styles including Oriental, southwestern, Italian, German, and American.

Taco Bender
467 North Main - (801) 259-6365

The Taco Bender is fast food that is not so fast. From tacos to burgers - they can fill the space in your stomach. They also serve breakfast from

7:00 AM until 10:30 AM. Don't ask me why, but they also have three drive-up windows.

Westerner Grill
331 North Main - (801) 259-9918

The Westerner is Moab's original diner. Open 24 hours, they are still serving the same food that they have been for many years. How they keep it fresh I just don't know.

Big Restaurant and Fast Food 'Chains'

Moab has its fair share of franchise fast food, and from what I hear, more are heading to town. This is part of the price of fame. The only positive thing that can usually be said about these places is that you usually get what you think you will get, and that can be good or bad.

Frosty Freeze - 396 South Main - (801) 259-7886
McDonalds - 640 South Main
Pizza Hut - 265 South Main - (801) 259-6345
Subway - 74 South Main - (801) 259-subs

Utah's Liquor Laws..!?

The state of Utah has some of the most unique and bazaar liquor laws in the nation. A degree in Government did little to prepare me to sort out the vagaries of the Utah Liquor Laws. However, for the benefit of the many travelers from out of state, here is my interpretation of the archaic statues.

First off, the State Liquor store at 260 South Main Street is the only place in town where hard liquor, wine and beer with an alcohol content over 3.2% is available for sale. The store is open Monday through Saturday from 11 AM to 9 PM.

The beer found at grocery and convenience stores has a liquor content of 3.2% or lower. You will also only find 3.2 beer at various licensed locations such as taverns, the golf course, the bowling alley and various restaurants.

It really begins to get confusing when you get into mixed drinks. Some restaurants are licensed to serve mixed drinks and wine by the glass as long as they adhere to the state's food service requirements. In many cases, restaurants will have more than one liquor license that covers different parts of the establishment. You may be hanging at a restaurant's bar, yet you would not be able to order a mixed drink unless you sit at the restaurant proper and order a meal. Sounds confusing? It is.

One Utah law that does make sense is that they do not allow open containers in or about any motor vehicle. Also, a blood alcohol level of 0.08% is the maximum allowed before you are declared "under the influence". Do yourself and everyone else on the road a favor and do not drink and drive or for that matter, drink and bike.

City Market

Never in my dreams would I have ever thought that someday I would be writing about a supermarket. I still can't believe I am, but the City Market in Moab rightfully deserves more than just a passing note in a guide to Moab.

Although not geographically located in the center of town, it is in my mind the heart of the city relating to commercial activity for tourists. Your average Moab visitor will stop by the visitor center maybe once or twice, perhaps hit up the bike shops two or three times, but will probably make a journey to the City Market many times.

So what is the attraction of a supermarket? First off, I have to commend the management at City Market for keeping their prices very reasonable. Most grocery stores in tourist towns seem to think they have a license to steal and charge outrageous prices. Not so with City. Their prices are more than reasonable, and in some cases downright cheap.

Open 24 hours a day, the market is always a whirlwind of activity inside and out. The parking lot is often full of vehicles loaded with bikes, whitewater rafting gear or other toys of the outdoor set. The parking lot is frequently a staging area for campers and river runners. You will often see them packing ice chests and readying gear for upcoming adventures.

Inside, you will find an excellent bakery, one of the finer deli's I have encountered in a supermarket, well stocked salad bar, produce section that would make a California market proud, pharmacy and just about everything else that you would expect to find. Not only do they sell quantities of block and cube ice, but they also have the dry variety. In addition, you can cash checks, receive money via Western Union, have your film processed in an hour, obtain fishing or hunting licenses, buy stamps, make photo copies, ship packages, rent videos and even send flowers.

I usually find myself in City Market once if not twice in one day. I often stop by in the morning to hit the bakery for breakfast and for trail goodies (see garlic sticks below). Later in the day, I may return for general shopping to score camp food or if I am feeling lazy but don't want to eat at a restaurant, I will score my dinner at the deli or salad bar. It is very possible to eat well on the cheap at the City Market.

On the down side, some of their cashiers are slower than molasses, but that will just give you time to catch up on the latest tabloid exploits of Elvis and UFOs.

By the way, there is another supermarket in town. Best Value Foods is located just down the street from City. What can I say about Best Value Foods? It is an alternative place to shop, the cashiers are faster and it is certainly less crowded. But it just doesn't quite stand up to what City Market has to offer.

Garlic Bread Stick Junkies

On my first visit to Moab, I hit up City Market at the old location. While there I discovered their cheese and onion rolls. For only 15¢ each, these were a killer deal and everyday I headed off on my ride with a few of these tasty treats. On each subsequent visit, I was always sure to pick up a supply of the bargain buns.

A few trips back, however, my friend Heath discovered City Market's garlic bread sticks, also for a mere *15¢*. These babies were incredible and it wasn't long before everyone on our trip was hooked on a daily dose of these buttery delights. At first, we were buying four or five a day each, but before long, we were buying them by the dozen. Our van reeked of garlic and little plastic bags containing one or two day old garlic sticks were everywhere. For a while, we were surviving on PowerBars and garlic sticks. We knew that it couldn't go on forever. Eventually we would have to leave town and be cut off from our source. Yes, we would have to go cold turkey. It was a sad moment indeed when the last stick was consumed somewhere in the Nevada desert along Highway-50. A few days later, the last of the garlic residue, a less than subtle reminder of our trip, exited through our pores.

Bummers, Big and Small

All is not perfect in Moab, but where can you say it is? Just like anywhere else in the country, you will find crime, punishment and people getting lost and injured. But, compared to just about any city in the US, Moab is a very safe place. In this era of drive buy shootings, gangs and a general abundance of violence, it is actually a joy to realize that the worst crime you have to worry about is bike theft. Heading into the backcountry is where problems become more serious. Take heed of the warnings and be prepared.

Rip-offs

One bummer to be aware of is bike theft. Although it might not be occurring in epidemic proportions, bike rip-offs are a definite reality in Moab. There might not necessarily be a bike stolen every day, but some days see a slew of rip-offs. It depends on whether sleezeoids are in town and how careful riders are with their bikes.

Prevent this trip bummer by using some common sense and locking your bike up when appropriate. The most common theft is just grab and ride. Some dirt bag finds a bike leaning against the wall at a restaurant with no lock, looks around and if the coast is clear, steals your steed. You might not need to use a major lock for cruising around town during the day, but bring at least a small cable. The slightest protection will often deter most casual thefts.

I am also aware of bikes occasionally being stolen off the roofs of vehicles parked in motel parking lots. This is a lesser problem in the motels where you can keep an eye on your vehicle by parking in front of your room, or bringing your bikes inside. The worries are more real if you are staying in one of the motels, where you can not keep close tabs on your vehicle and bike. So you might want to pay a little closer attention. Most motels now offer lockable bike storage or will let you bring your bike into the room.

Support the establishments that cater to the mountain bikers needs. If a motel fails to provide a way to secure your bike, I suggest you tell them this policy is bogus, and unless they have the only available room in town, try finding somewhere else to stay.

Occasionally, a bike will be ripped off from a car while on city streets. The best way to prevent this is to always have a lock on your bikes; and whenever possible, park where you will be able to keep an eye on them.

Now, dont go into a panic about losing your bike. It does happen, but do what you can to prevent it from happening to you. Also, remember that it isnt just bikes that thieves are after. Occasionally, they are happy to take easily removable parts like seatposts and seats. My bud, Tharyn went to the movies one evening, and the next day he noticed that one of his brake mounts was removed and another one was part way out. He was lucky he didnt lose a brake.

On a similar note, there have also been reports of car break-ins at trailheads. This appears to be another random crime and is not rampant. The important thing is to not leave valuables in your car. If you must leave them in your car, keep them out of sight.

Bikers are not immune from the law

Another bummer, less severe but still a bummer, are citations. Several signs around town warn that traffic laws for bikes are strictly enforced. It does not appear that bicyclists are being picked on or singled out;

however, if the police see you running a red light or other infraction, you will be cited. The bottom line is if you want respect from motorists while biking the pavement, then you need to respect the traffic laws. The main violations cited are running traffic lights and stop signs, and biking at night without proper lights. What's the hurry anyway? Stop when you are supposed to and everyone will be better off for it.

Where the heck are we?

Near the top of the major bummer category is getting lost. You would think that with all the roads and landmarks it would be tough to get lost in the Moab area. Well, it may be, but it happens frequently. The Grand County Search and Rescue Team has rescued many wayward mountain bikers. As recently as the late 1980s Search and Rescue averaged about five rescues a year. More recently this has mushroomed to 60 - 100 rescues per year with mountain bikers constituting the vast majority of the lost or injured parties.

Some of these searches have been for bikers that were injured, but the majority of the rescues have been for clueless or semi-clueless riders that managed to lose their way. I am not saying everyone that gets lost falls into this clueless category. It is very possible to be armed with a map and compass and the knowledge of how to use them and still get disoriented. However, by having these tools and skills, you greatly increase the chance that you will be able to put yourself back on track.

If you are prepared for the backcountry, the worse scenario may be just having to spend the night out in the cold. Some tips for staying found include. . . .

* When possible, bike with someone that knows the route.
* Always carry a map and compass and know how to use them.
* Let someone know your intended route.
* Read the guidebook trail description or bring the book or a copy of the trail description with you.
* If you do not have much experience in the backcountry, take on an out and back ride rather than a loop. In theory, you will be able to retrace your route back to the trailhead.
* Remember that the terrain looks different coming than going, and you tend to notice much more when you are going uphill

rather than screaming downhill. It is a good practice to look back now and then to see the route from the reverse perspective.

* Stop at all or most intersections. For one, it is a good place to regroup and second, it will assist you in familiarizing yourself with the area so that you will be more capable of retracing your route.
* Give yourself ample time to complete the tour. Many searches have been initiated because riders started tours too late and found themselves on an unfamiliar road or trail after dark.

One final note on getting lost. Grand County Search and Rescue spends a good portion of their limited funds on retrieving lost mountain bikers. As the recipient of their services, you will be billed for the search. The only good news is that since almost all the searches involve ground vehicles, the bill is not astronomical. It will, however, put a good dent in your vacation funds.

Crash and Burn

Most mountain bikers are all too painfully aware that crashing is an inevitable aspect of our beloved sport. These endo moments are avoided like the plague, but when they do occur, the memories are cherished and are usually discussed with pride around the campfire or while downing a few after ride brews. Fortunately, most crashes result in nothing more than a few cuts and scrapes and occasionally a slightly bruised ego.

On the other hand, many of us have also spent some time in emergency rooms dealing with our own or our buddys more serious injuries. Due in large part to the sheer number of mountain bikers, Moab gets more than its fair share of mountain bike related injuries.

No doubt, with over 100,000 user days per year and the painfully hard slickrock landing surface, the Slickrock Trail leads the way. Injuries on this trail have become so commonplace during the Fat Tire Festival that an ambulance is stationed at the trailhead in anticipation of the next casualty.

If you are injured and in need of x-rays, stitches or other treatment go to the the ***Allen Memorial Hospital*** at 719 West 400 No. (259-7191). The folks at this facility are quite experienced in treating mountain bike casualties.

During most of the spring and fall seasons, Allen Memorial treats three or four mountain bikers a week with the majority of the cases being broken bones and cuts requiring stitches. During Fat Tire Festival, the number jumps to five bikers or more per day. On the rare occasion where a more serious injury occurs, an airlift to Saint Mary's Hospital in Grand Junction is required.

While it is not advisable to think about injuries while you are riding, you can do a few things to minimize the risks. These include. . .

- Always bike with a helmet!!!!
- Bike within your limits. To get better, you do need to push yourself now and then, but in a backcountry situation you might want to back off somewhat and not get in over your head. It is fun to go fast, but the faster you go, the greater the consequences in a crash.
- Give your bike a safety check before each ride. Make sure bolts are not loose, that your headset is adjusted and your cranks and pedals are not about to fall off. Most importantly, check your brakes to make sure they work and that the pads are seated properly on the rims.
- Someone in your party should carry a first aid kit and hopefully, a few of you will know the basics of wilderness first aid.

Water

Carrying enough water is always an important consideration on any mountain bike tour. It takes on even greater importance when biking in the desert. You cannot carry too much water on a warm day ride in desert country. I am constantly amazed when I see some dweb on the slickrock trail in the middle of the day with one small water bottle or in some cases none at all. (See "Rider Without a Clue"). Minimally, you need two water bottle cages mounted on your bike with the largest water bottles that will fit. You can also replace one cage with a Blackburn Bomber cage that allows you to carry a liter and a half bottle in place of a standard bottle.

Another option is to carry an extra water bottle in your fanny back. Some fanny packs have side pockets designed to carry water bottles. If not, use a leak-proof bottle and carry it in your pack. Better yet, get yourself a Camelback hydration system, a soft bladder system that allow the biker to carry several quarts of water in their backs like a thin backpack. This simple product is a major accessory for biking Moab. Despite, in my opinion, of several design flaws, this is a great product, I will never bike in Moab again without one.

The key to staying hydrated is to sip small amounts of liquid at every opportunity, not just when you are thirsty. Also, the downing of appropriate fluids before and after a ride is also critical. Begin tanking up first thing in the morning with water prior to your ride. Just drinking coffee in the morning will not cut it. And though beer is often an after ride ritual with many riders, it is important that you replace your bodies fluids with liquids other than alcohol as you wind down, since alcohol promotes dehydration.

Heat and Cold Related Emergencies

The desert environment is a land of extremes. This is exemplified by the temperature swings that can occur on any given day. You can swelter under a blazing sun during the afternoon and still have to huddle around the campfire in the evening to stay warm. Because of the temperature variations, you need to be aware of some of the possible medical problems that can occur.

Heat Cramps, Heat Exhaustion and Heat Stroke

These are all conditions that can occur due to overexposure to heat. All three conditions can occur while on a mountain bike tour on a hot or even a warm day.

Heat cramps are painful muscle spasms believed to be caused by a combination of body fluid and salt loss from overexertion. The victim's body temperature will remain normal though the skin will become moist. Although not a major problem, it can also be a warning sign that the victim might be in the early stages of a more serious heat related problem.

First aid for heat cramps is to rest and cool down. If possible, find some shade and drink fluids. You can also massage and stretch the cramped muscles. Rest, fluids and massage will usually take care of the problem. However, do not give the person salt tablets which at this point can often cause more harm than good. During the rest of the tour, watch this person for signs of more serious heat related illness.

Heat exhaustion is much more serious and is the most common form of heat related illness. It is caused by overexertion in hot conditions without replacing enough of the fluids lost to perspiration. Some of the symptoms include: normal, or below normal body temperature - cool, moist, pale or flushed skin - nausea - headache - dizziness - loss of energy. If caught in the early stages, this can usually be handled with rest in a cool place and fluid intake. At its most serious stage, the person might begin to vomit, experience an elevated temperature and begin to lose consciousness. Do not force this person to pedal out until after completely rested and rehydrated or this might progress to heat stroke.

Heat stroke is not as common, but is very serious and requires immediate medical attention. It can usually be avoided if the earlier warning signs are noticed and the person is treated with rest and fluids. During heat stroke, the bodys systems begin malfunctioning due to extreme heat and lack of body fluids. Sweating stops and the body temperature will rise dangerously fast. If this illness should occur, it is best to send someone for help and attempt to lower the body temperature with wet compresses.

The key to all three of these heat related problems is to drink sufficient liquids and to keep your body core temperature at a reasonable temperature. One tip to keeping hydrated and to ward off various heat related maladies is to take advantage of whatever shade you come across on the trail. Whenever possible, take breaks where there is shade rather than out under the sun. If, while biking, part of the road is in shade, steer toward the shadows. The various heat related illnesses result from an accumulation of factors. The more often you cool your body core, the less chance you have of coming down with a heat related illness.

Everyone in your group should be aware of these warning signs. If you are the leader of your pack, it is especially important that you watch out for your group. Keep the pace down so that everyone is comfortable.

Hypothermia

Hypothermia is one of the more common backcountry medical emergencies. This is a result of the body core dropping below 95° and can be deadly. Be aware that freezing temperatures are not required to cause this problem. One of the biggest contributors to hypothermia is getting rained on when not wearing the proper gear. Wet clothing, along with the wind chill created while biking can quickly bring down your body core temperature. Symptoms include uncontrolled shivering, irregular pulse, glassy stare, and a decreasing level of consciousness.

Unfortunately, most of the treatments for hypothermia are unavailable for the average backcountry biker. The treatment is to re-warm the victim with dry clothes and warm drinks and to get the victim into a warm environment.

Since most mountain bikers do not carry a stove, sleeping bag or a change of clothes, the key is prevention. By carrying the proper gear, one can generally handle most foul weather situations. See the "gearing up" section for tips on bike clothing and layering. Also, since hypothermia is usually brought on by a combination of cold and exhaustion, be sure to take plenty of breaks and to eat high energy foods such as PowerBars.

Approaching storms, be aware of possible flash floods.

Flash Floods

One of the potential hazards of biking or even camping in the desert canyon country is flash floods. The Moab area does not receive a large annual rainfall, but what it does get tends to come down in a hurry. Mountain bikers should always keep a close watch on the weather for impending storms. This holds especially true when traveling in or cutting across narrow drainage areas.

When setting up camp during periods of changeable weather, make sure that your tent is away from any major or minor drainages. I have seen tents floating in two feet of water near the Slickrock Trailhead immediately after a sudden downpour. It can seem mildly amusing until it happens to you. I also spoke to a camper that set his tent up near Wall Street on Highway 279. He returned to camp during the storm to find his tent flattened beneath a several hundred foot waterfall pouring out from the cliffs above.

What Creek Crossing?

We were on our second ***Full On Conditions*** *ride in a row. The day before, we had been hammered by the elements; but on this particular day, the weather gods were smiling upon us. Our destination was the White Rim Trail via the Potash Road. During almost all of our ascent we were surrounded by threatening skies, but wherever we went, a meager ray of sunlight followed.*

We eventually paused at the outstanding vista point below Dead Horse Point. Our original destination was ahead in the midst of a light and sound show. We decided to hang out for awhile to enjoy nature's fury from a distance and to see how the storm played out. If it would back off, then we would proceed. If not, then we would have an almost all downhill retreat awaiting us.

Within a half hour, our decision was made for us as the storm began bearing in. No worries. We had advance notice and with gravity on our side, we figured we could outrun the rain. Little did we know that the front had outflanked us and was lurking around the bend in ambush.

I had been hanging in the back of the pack with two other riders when the rains hit. We paused for a moment and put on the rain gear. I took off ahead and let my bike run until I came to a dry creek bed. I cruised over the small rock garden and then charged up the short rise on the other side. At the top, I waited for Ken and Jackie.

They were only a few minutes behind, but when they came up to me, one of them said, "I didn't remember that creek crossing on the way in."

"What creek crossing?" was my response.

"The one 50 yards back."

Apparently, within a few minutes, the little ravine had gone from a dry creek bed to a one and one half foot deep foaming creek. I was duly impressed.

Things that bite and sting

When you mention the desert to certain city slickers, the first thing that comes to mind is rattlesnakes and scorpions. Well, the desert country of Southeastern Utah does have both, but don't lose any sleep worrying about them. Daytime rattlesnake sightings are infrequent and the bite of the local scorpions can be painful, but certainly not deadly unless you are highly allergic to insect bites. Chances are you will see neither of these critters. More than likely, your encounters will be with mosquitoes, flies and no-see-ums. Although these buggers will generally leave you alone during the middle of the day, be sure to bring along some bug repellent to foil their early and late feeding time.

Burn Baby Burn

Besides dehydration, another consideration when biking in the high desert is sunburn. The 4000 feet elevation and the absence of shade can contribute to bad sunburns along the Moab trails. For many, this might just mean becoming a redneck with rosy legs; but for those that bike shirtless or with tanktops, this can be pretty painful.

This is easily remedied by keeping your shirt on and lathering up exposed parts with sunscreen with SPF factor of at least 15. Also, since shade can be scarce, plan your longer breaks to coincide with the appearance of a nice chunk of shade.

The Biker Without A Clue

We are half way along the outer loop on the Slickrock Trail. Our brains are parboiling under the mid-day desert sun and we are hammered. For such a short ride, this true "classic" can be brutal to all of us mere mortal mountain biker types. My buds and I are hanging out trying to muster up the energy to continue on. Of course, we are not letting on to each other that we are hammered, but it is obvious to all. We munch our PowerBars and sip from our depleted water rations when along comes the "rider without a clue".

We all give him half a glance and mutter a polite hello, as most riders are attuned to do along the trail. He pulls up and says in a raspy voice, "Dudes, where does this trail go? Can I get back to the parking lot heading this way?"

This instantly gets our attention. Here we are, on the most famous mountain bike trail in the world and this guy does not have the slightest idea what he has gotten himself into.

A closer inspection revealed that this Waldo had no helmet, water bottles, shirt, sunscreen, tools, and obviously- brain cells. What he did have was a sunburn that allowed him to blend in with the red sandstone like a chameleon not to mention one heck of a thirst. The guy was turning into a prune before our eyes. How he had gotten this far I will never know.

Normally, when finding a rider in distress, we go out of our way to help. We might offer directions, a dab of sunscreen, an extra PowerBar, a spare tube, mechanical assistance, first aid, or at least encouragement, but this guy needed everything. We figured he was only entitled to one of the above or else we might be interfering with the Darwinian theory on natural selection, so we gave him the word on the shortest route to the trailhead. We shook our heads in amazement as he rattled off down the trail under the watchful eyes of a circling group of buzzards. Suddenly, we didn't feel quite as hungry, thirsty and tired. For the rest of the ride, the group mantra that kept us going was "at least, we are not the rider without a clue."

Canyonlands Fat Tire Festival

Every year, the biggest influx of mountain bikers in Moab occurs during the Fat Tire Festival. Since 1985, this event has been held during the last week of October and unofficially ends the year of mountain biking in Moab. (In reality, if you ask the locals, they will tell you that some outstanding biking without crowds can be enjoyed in November if you don't mind the short days and cooler weather.)

Depending on your likes and dislikes, the Canyonlands Fat Tire Festival is either the best time to visit Moab or one of the worst. Thousands of mountain bikers descend on Moab for the festival. Many have paid the registration fees that range from $45 to $80 to become official event participants, while hundreds of unregistered riders are there to enjoy the scene from the periphery.

Overshadowed in recent years by many of the big NORBA National and World Championship Races in drawing crowds, the CFTF maintains its tradition as a participatory event for the masses. Instead of big time spectator races, the CFTF is geared toward riding the Moab backcountry, with some in-town partying thrown in for good measure.

Despite the lack of competition, except the bike rodeo, poker run and World Bicycle Polo Championships, the festival is still a major annual gathering for folks from all aspects of the mountain bike industry. Big time racers, magazine writers, industry reps and Joe average mountain bikers have ride side by side on the roads and trails. Manufacturers, from the top national brands as well as garage and basement inventors, are on hand to talk shop, test their wares, and to get instant feedback from consumers on their latest widgets and gizmos.

The focus of the event is riding. Every day of the festival, guided rides of various difficulties are led, while in the evening programs ranging from slide shows to live music are presented. The week's festivities are capped off with the annual Halloween Costume Party.

So should you attend the festival? You might want to consider it if you enjoy the idea of taking over the town and hob nobbing with large numbers of other mountain bikers and industry representatives. You might also consider the festival if you have yet to develop good route finding skills. It is better to take the guided rides than to chance getting lost in the outback.

On the other hand, this might not be what you are looking for in a backcountry biking vacation. Are you prepared for people everywhere, campsites and motels full, and long waits at the restaurants.

I personally know people that have gone to the festival once. Did it - been there - but once was enough. Their next Moab trip will be during some other time. On the other hand, I also know several bikers that return every year.

If you would like information on the next Canyonlands Fat Tire Festival, contact the event organizers, ***Canyon Country Cyclists*** at 94 West 100 North, Moab, UT 84532, or call ***Rim Cyclery*** at (801) 259-5333.

Calendar of Events

Some of the more popular annual events are listed below. Some of these might lure you to Moab while others will give you a good idea of when not to come. The dates for most of the events vary from year to year so check with the Moab Information Center for specific dates.

January

- Winter Festival

March

- Canyonland Half Marathon - this event lures almost 1000 competitors so most of the local lodging gets booked up well in advance.

April

- Outdoor Photography
- Annual Jeep Safari - Moab's biggest yearly event is held during Easter Vacation.
- Moab Rocks and Road - these bike races are part of the Cannondale Cup Fat Tire Series. Besides the races there are also daily guided tours.

May

- Arts Festival

July

- Grand Old 4th of July Celebration

August

- Grand County Fair

September

- Labor Day Jeep Campout - another busy weekend
- Music Festival

October

- Red Rock Gem and Mineral Show
- Canyonlands Fat Tire Festival

Alternative Entertainment

Mountain biking is the lure that gets you to Moab, but once you are there, is mountain biking going to be your sole recreational pursuit? For some, the answer is yes, but for many, other forms of amusement or sightseeing will probably be in order. The following is a listing of alternative recreation possibilities for Moab travelers.

River Floats and Whitewater Rafting

With the Colorado River flowing on the edge of town and the Green River not too far away, it is no wonder that rafting is a popular local pastime. Whether you want the excitement of whitewater or the tranquil beauty of a casual flat water float beneath the majestic sandstone canyon walls, there is a local outfitter that will take care of your needs.

Offerings range from half day floats near town to multi-day adventures. You can choose to experience the rivers as a participant on a paddle boat or canoe or leave the work to someone else in an oar guided raft or motor powered raft or boat.

While there are many companies from outside of Moab that run river tours on the Colorado and Green Rivers. I have chosen to list just the local companies.

These are the ones that you will more than likely deal with once you are in Moab:

Adrift Adventures
378 North Main - (801) 259-8594

Canyon Voyages
352 North Main - (801) 259-6007

Colorado River Tours - Colorado River Bridge
North Highway 191 - (801) 259-2628

Downstream River Works
401 North Main - (801) 259-4121

Griffith River Expeditions
2231 South Highway 191 - (801) 259-8229

Moab Rafting Company
PO Box 801 - (801) 259-RAFT

NAVTEC Expeditions
321 North Main - (801) 259-7983

North American River Expeditions
543 North Main - (801) 259-5865

Red River Canoe Company
497 North Main - (801) 259-7722

River Runner Sports
401 North Main - (801) 259-4121

Slickrock Adventures
PO Box 1400 - (801) 259-6996

Tag-A-Long Travel
452 North Main - (801) 259-8946

Tex's River Ways
691 North 500 West - (801) 259-5101

World Wide River Expeditions
625 North Sands Rd - (801) 259-7515

Rock Climbing

The canyon walls and rock spires surrounding Moab make for some interesting climbing. Routes abound, but one of the more popular areas are along the walls on Highway-279. This area is refereed to as "*Wall Street*" and during the peak season you might see over a dozen belay stations set up in the beautiful stretch of road along the Colorado River. Another famous climbing site is the *Fisher Towers*, northeast of Moab off of Highway 128. The towers draw many climbers from all over the country.

Global Expeditions, located at 3071 South Highway 191 - (801)259-6604 offers a climbing school based out of Moab from April 15 until October 15. Another source of information on climbing is Rim Cyclery, which also carries a complete line of climbing gear and local guidebooks.

Hiking

Hiking can be a nice way to spend all or part of a day in Moab. Getting off the bike and taking a hike can be a nice change of pace from the rigors of mountain biking. Hoofing along the trail allows you to work different muscles or perhaps let that sore butt have a day out of the saddle. Hiking with proper rain gear can also be a great way to spend a foul weather day if you don't want to take on the elements with your bike. On these foul weather days you can have many of the best hikes in Arches National Park almost to yourself. It sure beats sharing the trails with busloads of bermuda short clad tourists.

Some of the most amazing sights in Arches and Canyonlands National Parks are only open to hikers. Although all paved and most dirt roads are open to mountain bikes, the trails are not. This doesn't mean that you have to forgo seeing the incredible scenery. Lock up your bike, put on some hiking boots or running shoes and spend some time hoofing the backcountry. Hikes range from long backpack routes to short roadside walks.

If a short walk around town is more to your liking, pick up a copy of the *"Moab Area Historic Walking Tour"* at the Information Center. This self guided tour begins at the Dan O'Laurie Museum and proceeds to guide you to the oldest building in town and gives you a short historical background for each.

Also at the Information Center, you can pick up a free copy of the *"Moab Area Hiking Trails"* brochure which guides you to eight short hiking routes.

Up, Up and Away

Wild West Balloon Company
401 North Main Street - (801) 259-9000

Wild West features a variety of scenic desert hot-air balloon flights from April through the end of October.

National Parks

Although mountain biking is restricted to paved and dirt roads in the National Parks, they are still merit a visit. Whether you decide to bike the roads, tour in your car, or hike some of the trails, you will enjoy these national treasures.

Arches National Park is the closest to Moab and should be on your must visit list. The entrance and visitor center is located five miles north of town on Highway-191. The visitor center is open from 8:00 AM to 4:30 PM daily. For information call (801)259-8161.

The **Island in the Sky District in Canyonlands National Park** is 35 miles from Moab and the location of the famous White Rim Trail. Although the Island in the Sky is actually southwest of Moab, you have to head north on Highway 191 and then cut over on Utah State Route 313 to get there. The visitor center is located two miles inside the park boundry. The phone number is (801)259-4351.

The Needles and the Maze district are both far from Moab (80 and 140 miles). For up-to-date information call the **Needles District office** at (801)259-4711 and the **Maze District office** at (801)259-2652.

Horseback Rides

Old West Trail Rides - (801) 259-7410 - located nine miles south of Moab on Highway 191. Old West offers an evening ride and dine from March through the end of October. Guests are taken on a two hour evening ride. The night is capped with a Dutch oven cookout. The cost is $30.

Horse rentals by the hour is another option available.

Auto Tours

If you are not up to riding one day, hop in your car and take a scenic cruise. Some great destinations to visit in your motor-vehicle include the National Parks or the La Sal Mountain Loop.

An interesting auto tour is outlined in a pamphlet distributed by the Moab Visitor Center. The *"Moab Area Rock Art Auto Tour"* guides you to several roadside sites with easily accessible Indian Rock Art. Both petroglyphs and pictographs are visible at these five unique sites. Another free brochure distributed by the Information Center that you might want to pick up is *"Moab Area Self Guided Auto Tours,"* which guides you along the Colorado Riverway, Arches and Canyonlands National Parks, Dead Horse Point State Park, the La Sal Mountain Loop Road and Canyon Rims Recreation Area.

If you have not been to Arches National Park, then no long visit to Moab should conclude without at least a drive through of this park. Arches National Park makes for a great destination during inclement weather as the dramatic skies contrast wonderfully with the red rock canyon walls. If you have your rain gear along, you will also be able to hike some of the short walks to arches without crowds of other tourists.

One final tour outlined in a free Information Center brochure is the "Moab Area Movie Locations Auto Tour." By following this route you can see locations used in many of the movies filmed near Moab.

Showtime

Slickrock Cinemas 3
580 Kane Creek Blvd - (801) 259-4441

Since the demise of the local drive-in, catching first run movies was not possible in Moab. This has recently been remedied with the opening of this new air-conditioned theater. The Slickrock Cinemas is open year round and features three screens. I suggest, however, that you do not leave your bike on your car rack while attending the show.

Canyonlands By Night
Colorado River and Highway 191 - (801) 259-5261

Talk about a show with staying power. Canyonlands By Night has been presenting this spectacular "sight and sound" show on the Colorado River for over 25 years. You can catch the sunset cruise on the Moab Queen and watch the canyon walls come to life with the illumination of over 40,000 watts of light. This program is offered May through October.

Canyon's Edge

Moab Information Center
Center and Main

The Canyon's Edge is a multi-projector slide presented by the Canyonlands Natural History Association and shown at the Moab Information Center. This award winning program features images of spectacular landscapes, ancient ruins, natural history and more. Canyon's Edge is shown twice daily from April through October. Showtimes vary, so check with the information center for times. The cost is $4 for adults, $3 for seniors and $2 for children under 12.

Museums

I consider the entire Moab region to be one large geologic museum, however, the pickings are slim for indoor museum hounds. What you will find can add to the pleasure of your vacation.

The Dan O'Laurie Museum
118 East Center Street - (801) 259-7985

I highly recommend that you make some time though you won't need much to take in the Dan O'Laurie Museum. The price certainly is right (free) and the exhibits certainly adds to your local knowledge of

Moab's history, geology and archaeology. I was particularly fascinated by the more recent history of the uranium boom of the 1950s and 60s. In addition to the exhibits on the main floor, the works of local artisans are shown at the upstairs gallery. The museum is open Monday through Saturday from 1:00 to 5:00 PM and 7:00 to 9:00 PM and closed on Sundays.

The Hollywood Stuntmen's Hall of Fame
100 East 100 North - (801) 259-6100

No visit to Moab would be complete without a visit to the Hollywood Stuntmen's Hall of Fame. If you are a fan of the movies, than you should take some time and visit this unique museum featuring relics and photos from many of the greatest stunts and stuntmen and women of all time. The Hall is the labor of love of owner and curator and former stuntman John Hagner who has been collecting movie memorabilia for over 25 years. Some of the displays include those for movies filmed in the Moab area. Admission is $3 for adults, $2 for seniors, and $1 for children 3-12. The Hall of Fame is open weekdays 10:00 AM to 7:00 PM and weekends noon to 6:00 PM.

Grand County Library
25 South 100 East - (801) 259-5421

Although not a museum you can still learn about local history, geology, etc, by cruising the stacks at the library.

Air Tours

Interested in a whole new perspective of Moab and the National Parks that surround it? Take to the air with one of the companies that offer scenic flyovers of the Canyonlands National Park and beyond. From the air in either a fixed wing aircraft or a helicopter you will be able to see your mountain bike routes from an entirely new light.

Red Tail Aviation
Canyonlands Field - (800)842-9251 - (801) 259-7421

Red Tail has been in operation since 1978. They offer one hour flights over Canyonlands *($60)* and two hour flights that also take in Capitol Reef National Park, Lake Powell and other sights.

Mountain Flying Service
321 N. Main - (801) 259-8050

Mountain Flying Service offers a variety of scenic flights ranging from their one hour Canyonlands tour *($60)* to longer tours that take in many of the surrounding sights.

Arches Helicopters
1301 1/2 Highway 191 - (801) 259-4637

Arches Helicopters offers scenic fly-overs similar to the fixed wing operations. In addition, they also cater to bikers with heli-biking. Arches Helicopters will air-lift you and a few lazy buddies to any number of drop-off points to begin a day of descent. Not cheap.

Slickrock Air Guides
2231 South Highway 191 - (801) 259-6216

Slickrock Air Guides also offer a one-hour Canyonlands fly-over for a *$6* per person fee.

Golf

Moab Golf Course - 2750 South East Bench Road - (801) 259-6488

The Moab Golf Course is open to the public and features a challenging 18 hole course. The lush green fairways offer quite a contrast to the red rock formations that surround the course. The Moab Golf course has just about everything you would expect to find such as a driving range, club rentals, pro shop and a restaurant.

Winery

Arches Vineyards
2182 South Highway 191 - (801) 259-5397

A wine tasting room in Moab? Hard to believe, but it does exist. Arches Winery is a recent addition to the economy of Moab, producing fine wines from local grapes. Fifteen growers are currently supplying the grapes for the operation which has expanded their capacity from 1500 gallons in 1989 to almost 17,000 gallons in 1993. Currently, the wine tasting room is open Monday through Saturday, excluding holidays.

Bowling Anyone?

Moab Lanes

1145 South Highway 191 - (801) 259-5188

If you like to wear smelly rental bowling shoes and take in second hand smoke, then the Moab Lanes might be the place for you. Enter the air-conditioned comfort of the 12 lane bowling alley for a definite alternative to mountain biking. Moab Lanes is open seven days a week from noon to 11:00 PM most of the year. From June until mid-August they close on Sundays.

Four Wheel Drive Rentals

Since mountain bikers have their own way of exploring the backcountry without the aid of gasoline powered vehicles, I don't expect there is much need for 4x4 rentals. However, you never know when the urge or need to head into the backcountry with one of these vehicles might hit, so here is a list of available 4x4 rentals.

Canyonlands 4x4 Rentals
550 North Main - (801) 259-4567

Canyonlands 4x4 offers rentals and guided tours. Their fleet includes Jeep Wranglers, Ford Explorers and trucks. Free maps and trail information is also available.

Farabee 4x4 Rentals
234 North Main - (801) 259-7494

Farabee stable of four wheel drives feature Jeep Wranglers and Cherokees.

Slickrock Jeep Rentals
284 North Main - (801) 259-5678

Thrifty Car Rental
711 South Main (in the Moab Valley Inn) - (801) 259-7317

Thrifty - Redtail Aviation
Canyonlands Airport - (801 259-7421

Thrifty has 4x4 sport vehicles as well as sedans, convertibles, vans and small trucks.

There are numerous guidebooks available for the four wheel drive set and you can also pick up a free copy of *"Moab Area Jeep Trails"* at the Moab Information Center.

Sports Nuts

Center Court Restaurant and Sports Bar
686 South Main - (801) 259-2524

Moab is the land of participatory sports, but for those of us that also enjoy watching our favorite teams battle it out on the tube, we now have a sports bar to retreat to. I have to warn you Center Court is in the minor leagues of sport bars. I recently experienced a major let-down, when the featured NFL game of the week with my 49ers was preempted at Center Court for an infomercial. Bogus.

Shopping

For you shop until you drop types, you must be forewarned that you will not find any malls in Moab. You will find many shops ranging from tacky souvenirs, rocks, southwestern art, cowboy art, tee-shirts, books, Indian crafts, clothing, and just about everything else you would expect to find in a southwestern tourist town.

There are three great bike shops in town with state of the art gear, accessories and clothing available. Make sure to visit this shops and mentioned that I told you should shop there.

For the Kids

Beat the Heat

King World Water Park
1500 North Highway 191 - (801) 259-2837

A recent letter to the editor in one of the mountain bike magazines lamented the fact that Moab was getting too commercial. The greatest offender referred to was the new water park. Obviously, this letter writer does not have kids. It may be tacky, but King World offers an opportunity for the kids to hang out and play on the water slides and swimming pools. It may be hokey, but it helps to beat the heat.

Fishing

Portal Fishery
1261 No Highway 191 - (801) 259-6108

Well, it ain't exactly 'The River Runs Through It', but if you are desperate for some fishing, look no further than the Portal Fishery. No license is required and if you don't have your own gear, they will provide you with fishing tackle.

Yagottawasanna Go Cart and Family Fun Center
600 West Cedar (behind McDonalds) 259-8007

The Family Fun Center offers go cart racing as well as pool, fooseball and video games.

Other Business services

Reservations is their business

There are two operators in Moab that can book your lodging and all your recreational needs.

Arches Reservations Central
76 South Main - (800)778-4737 or (801)259-4737

Moab/Canyonlands Central Reservations
(801)259-5125

Miscellaneous Visitor Services

The Moab area code is *(801)* and the zip code is *84532*

Emergency Services

For all emergencies having to do with fire, police or medical, call 9-1-1.

Moab Police Department
121 East Center - (801) 259-8938

Grand County Sheriff and Search and Rescue
125 East Center - (801) 259-8115

Allen Memorial Hospital
719 West 400 North, Moab - (801) 259-7191

Information and Reservation Services

Visitor Center
Center and Main - (801) 259-8825

Moab Travel Council
200 North 100 West - (801) 259-8825 or (800) 635-6622

Moab/Canyonlands Central Reservations
92 East Center - (801) 259-5125

Moab Chamber of Commerce
805 North Main - (801) 259-7814

Canyon Country Activity Center
PO Box 1326 - (801) 259-7303

Land Managers

Bureau of Land Management
Moab District 82
East Dogwood Ave - (801) 259-6111

Grand Resource Area
885 South Sand Flats Road - (801) 259-8193

Colorado River Program
885 South Sand Flats Road - (801) 259-442

Forest Service
Manti-La Sal National Forest

Moab Ranger District
125 West 200 South - (801) 259-7155

Monticello Ranger District
587-2041

National Park Service

Arches National Park
(801) 259-8161

Canyonlands National Park
Information - (801) 259-7164
Headquarters - (801) 259-3911
Island in the Sky District - (801) 259-4351
Maze District - (801) 259-2652
Needles District - (801) 259-6568

National Bridges National Monument
(801) 259-5174

State Parks and Recreation

Southeastern Region Office
1165 South Highway 191 - (801) 259-8151

Dead Horse Point State Park
(801) 259-2614

State Park Reservations
(800) 322-3770

Copying and duplication services

Canyonlands Copy Center
59 South Main #3 - (801) 259-8431

Full service copy facilities. Open daily from 8:00 am to 6:00 pm

Other photocopies can be made at copy machines at a variety of locations in town including City Market and Family Drug.

Photo Processing and Supplies

Moab Photo Lab
64 South Main - (801) 259-4181
Complete photo lab can handle any processing needs.

Spencer's Printing and Stationers
284 South Main - (801) 259-5735

Westlight Photography
750 South Main - (801) 259-7943
Professional photo lab that offers color and black and white services.

Bookstores and Maps

Back of Beyond Books
83 North Main - (801) 259-5154
Excellent bookstore where many hours can be spent browsing the stacks. Excellent selection of local books and guides.

Canyonlands Natural History Association
30 South 100 East - (801) 259-6003
Great selection of books on local topics.

Osborns Books and Magazines
50 S. Main - (801) 259-2665

Osborns is other fine bookstore just down the street a short distance from Back of Beyond Books. If you can't find what you want at Back of Beyond, you will probably find it here.

Maps, Etc
29 East Center - (801) 259-7741

Excellent selection of guidebooks, specialty and USGS topo maps.

Moab Information Center
Corner of Center and Main

The Moab Information center is an excellent source for local books and maps. It is also a clearing house for information from the Park Service, BLM, Forest Service and Moab information services. Centrally located in the heart of town, you can also come here for upto date weather reports and forecasts, campground information and displays. You should also try to catch their award winning multi-media slide presentation, The Canyon's Edge.

Money Needs

Banks

First Security Bank
4 North Main

Located at the corner of Main and Center, they also have an ATM facing main street.

First Western National bank
300 S. Main - (801) 259-5961

ATM - Cash

If you need cash you might want to try the City Market. They have an ATM, they can cash checks, and they also have a Western Union counter.

Pet Care

Adobe Creek Animal Hospital
350 South 400 East - (801) 259-6360

Moab Veterinary Clinic
4575 Spanish Valley Dr - (801) 259-8710

Spanish Valley Veterinary Clinic
1428 Spanish Valley Dr - (801) 259-5216

Vet-Art
180 South 200 East Main - (801) 259-8777

Rental Cars and 4WD

Canyonlands 4X4 Rentals
550 N. Main - (801) 259-4567

Farabee 4x4 Rentals
234 N. Main - (801) 259-7494

Slickrock Jeep Rentals
284 N. Main - (801) 259-5678

Thrifty Car Rental
16 S. Main - (801) 259-7317

Taxi or Bike Shuttle

Dial Two Five Nine-Taxi Shuttle
21 Williams Trailer Ct (801) 259-8294

Only in Moab will you see bike racks on a taxi. Two Five Nine-Taxi provides a shuttle service for mountain bikers to the various trailheads around town. Common shuttles include Porcupine Rim, Gemini Bridges, the top of the Shafer Trail and the La Sals.

Babysitting Services

There is limited child care available Monday through Friday on a space available basis.

Community Child Care Center
544 N. MiVida Dr - (801) 259-6984

Jaspers Day Care
90 North 400 East - (801) 259-5483

Hospital

Allen Memorial Hospital
719 West 400 North - (801) 259-7191

Post Office

50 East 100 North - (801) 259-7427

Laundromat

Moab Speedqueen Laundromat
702 South Main - (801) 259-7456

Showers

If you wash your clothes, you might as well wash your body. The locations have pay per shower facilities. Prices vary.

Canyonlands Campark - 555 South Main
Edge of the Desert - 1251 South Millcreek Dr.
Holiday Haven RV Park - 400 North 500 West
Lazy Lizard Hostel - 1231 South Highway 191
Moab KOA - 3225 South Highway 191
Moab Valley RV & Campark - 1773 North Highway 191
Packcreek Campark - 1520 Murphy Lane
Poison Spider Bicycle Shop - 497 North Main
Portal RV Park and Fishery
Slickrock Campground - 1301 1/2 North Main
Spanish Trail RV and Campark - 2980 South Highway 191
Up the Creek Campground - 210 East 300 South

Massage

Wind down after a tough ride with a relaxing and theraputic massage.

Trail Head Sports Massage
88 West Center - (801) 259-2905
Call for appointment.

Roots Bodywork Company
11 North Main #9 - (801) 259-5610
By appointment only. Rates range from $40 for the one hour regular session to $70 for their two hour Ultimate Session

Grocery Stores

City Market
425 South Main - (801) 259-5181

Moab Best Value Foods
702 South Main - (801) 259-5695

State Liquor Store

260 South Main - (801) 259-5314

Pharmacies

City Market
425 South Main - (801) 259-8971

Family Drug
90 North Main - (801) 259-7771

Walker Drug
290 South Main - (801) 259-5959

Media

Newspaper

Times/Independent
35 East Center - (801) 259-4897

The Canyon Country Zephyr
P.O. Box 327 - (801) 259-7773

KZMU Moab Public Radio
P.O. Box 1076 - (801) 259-4897

Recycling

There are several locations where you can take your cans, bottles and a few other items to be recycled.

City Market - aluminum, glass, newspaper and tin can.

Poison Spider Bikes - aluminum, glass, newspaper, tin cans and cardboard.

Slickrock trailhead - aluminum cans and bottles.

Recycling center on the way to the Slickrock Trail - aluminum, glass, newspaper, cardboard and tin cans.

Waste Disposal

The Moab dumb is located on the Sand Flats Road on the way to the Slickrock Trail. Outside Magazine gave this facility the title of "*America's Most Scenic Dump.*" I totally agree. You can drop off your garbage at this site. There is even an area where can leave your solid waste marked "*Outfitters*".

TRIP PLANNING GUIDE

Date: ______________________________ To ___________________________

Number in Party ____________________

Conveyance ____

Airline Reservation ____

____

Car Reservation ____

____

Hotel Reservation ____

____

Equipment Reservation ____

____

____

____

Itinerary ____

____

____

____

____

____

____

____

____

____

____

TRIP PLANNING GUIDE

Date: ______________________________ To ___________________________

Number in Party ____________________

Conveyance ____

Airline Reservation____

____

Car Reservation ____

____

Hotel Reservation____

____

Equipment Reservation ____

____

____

____

Itinerary ____

____

____

____

____

____

____

____

____

____

____

TRIP PLANNING GUIDE

Date: ______________________________ To ___________________________

Number in Party ____________________

Conveyance ____

Airline Reservation____

____

Car Reservation ____

____

Hotel Reservation____

____

Equipment Reservation____

____

____

____

Itinerary ____

____

____

____

____

____

____

____

____

____

____

TRIP PLANNING GUIDE

Date: ______________________________ To ___________________________

Number in Party ____________________

Conveyance ____

Airline Reservation ____

____

Car Reservation ____

____

Hotel Reservation ____

____

Equipment Reservation ____

____

____

____

Itinerary ____

____

____

____

____

____

____

____

____

____

____

TRIP PLANNING GUIDE

Date: ______________________________ To ______________________________

Number in Party ____________________

Conveyance ____

Airline Reservation ____

____

Car Reservation ____

____

Hotel Reservation ____

____

Equipment Reservation ____

____

____

____

Itinerary ____

____

____

____

____

____

____

____

____

____

____

TRIP PLANNING GUIDE

Date: ______________________________ To ___________________________

Number in Party ____________________

Conveyance ____

Airline Reservation____

____

Car Reservation ____

____

Hotel Reservation____

____

Equipment Reservation____

____

____

____

Itinerary ____

____

____

____

____

____

____

____

____

____

____

TRIP PLANNING GUIDE

Date: ______________________ To ______________________

Number in Party ______________

Conveyance ______________________________________

Airline Reservation ______________________________________

____

Car Reservation ______________________________________

____

Hotel Reservation ______________________________________

____

Equipment Reservation ______________________________________

____

____

____

Itinerary ______________________________________

____

____

____

____

____

____

____

____

____

____

TRIP PLANNING GUIDE

Date: ______________________________ To ___________________________

Number in Party ____________________

Conveyance ____

Airline Reservation____

____

Car Reservation ____

____

Hotel Reservation____

____

Equipment Reservation____

____

____

____

Itinerary ____

____

____

____

____

____

____

____

____

____

____

TRIP PLANNING GUIDE

Date: ______________________ To ______________________

Number in Party ______________

Conveyance ______________________________________

Airline Reservation ______________________________________

____

Car Reservation ______________________________________

____

Hotel Reservation ______________________________________

____

Equipment Reservation ______________________________________

____

____

____

Itinerary ______________________________________

____

____

____

____

____

____

____

____

____

____

TRIP PLANNING GUIDE

Date: ______________________________ To __________________________

Number in Party ____________________

Conveyance ____

Airline Reservation____

____

Car Reservation ____

____

Hotel Reservation____

____

Equipment Reservation ____

____

____

____

Itinerary ____

____

____

____

____

____

____

____

____

____

____

Other Mountain N'air Books:

Best Day Hikes of the California Northwest, The – Art Bernstein
ISBN: 1-879415-02-X $13.50

Best Hikes of the Trinity Alps (CA) – Art Bernstein
ISBN: 1-879415-05-4 $17.00

Cross Country-NORTHEAST– John Fitzgerald
ISBN: 1-879415-07-0 $12.00

Cross Country Skiing in Southern California – Eugene Mezereny
ISBN: 1-879415-08-9 $14.00

Great Rock Hits of Hueco Tanks – Paul Piana
ISBN: 1-879415-03-8 $ 6.95

High Endeavors – Pat Ament
ISBN: 1-879415-00-3 $12.95

Los Angeles Hikes and Trails, Volume 1– Eugene Mezereny
ISBN: 1-879415-10-0 $17.00

On Mountains & Mountaineers – Mikel Vause
ISBN:1-879415-06-2 $12.95

Portland Hikes – Bernstein/Jackman
ISBN: 1-879415-09-7 $18.00

Rock and Roses – Mikel Vause, ed.
ISBN: 1-879415-01-1 $11.95

The Rogue River Guide – Kevin K. Tice
ISBN: 1-879415-12-7 $15.00